STAR ☆ BOOKS

# Congregationalists and Unity

BY

ERIK ROUTLEY

*Minister of Augustine-Bristo Congregational Church, Edinburgh*

LONDON

A. R. MOWBRAY & Co. LIMITED

First published in 1962

PRINTED IN GREAT BRITAIN BY
A. R. MOWBRAY & CO. LIMITED IN THE CITY OF OXFORD
2323

## INTRODUCTION

BY THE BISHOP OF BRISTOL

ONE of the most encouraging facts of recent years, for all those who care about Christian unity, is the undoubted growth in prayer for it. All over Christendom, we are beginning to acknowledge our debt to the Abbé Paul Couturier, the humble schoolmaster-priest of Lyon, who taught us all to pray, with greater persistence and greater charity, that all God's people might become one "when He wills and by the means which He wills." The ever-increasing demand for the literature which accompanies the Week of Prayer for Christian Unity (January 18th–25th each year) is a token of something too deep for measurement yet significant in itself. The popular imagination was caught by the personality of Pope John XXIII and the visit which Archbishop Fisher of Canterbury paid to him, an event which aroused interest in circles little concerned, as a rule, with ecclesiastical affairs. The Assembly of the World Council of Churches at New Delhi and the second Vatican Council in Rome both assist to keep the idea of Christian Unity hovering on the edge of many minds. In the wide area that lies between the persistent prayer of the committed and the sporadic interest of the average newspaper-reader or televiewer there is abundant need for *information* at many levels of seriousness, from the specialized theological treatise to the popular interpretation of our separated yet related traditions.

Within that wide territory, this series of books seeks to

serve those who are sufficiently interested to wish to know how representatives of the main traditions in these islands view the prospects for unity. The writers are "representative" in the sense that each of them is a loyal and active member of his own communion and alert to ecumenical questions, but not in the sense that any one of them would claim for what he writes an authority more than that of personal opinion. Each of them has tried to face "the Hard Facts of Unity" and to give his own response to them.[1]

One of the greatest needs in ecumenical discussion is the building-up of a common vocabulary in which to converse. The differences between the books in this series will show how far we have yet to go. But behind that need lies the deeper one of a common frame of reference. It is an inevitable, though exasperating, consequence of our separated traditions that we can never be sure when we mean the same things by different words or different things by the same words, for we use our words within a total context which colours their meaning. The most elementary and fundamental instance is the variety of meanings and shades of meaning in the words "unity," "union," "re-union," with the implications they carry for the relation of "spiritual" to "visible," of "unity" to "uniformity," of "history" to "eschatology" and much besides. At the New Delhi Assembly, the most notable achievement of the Unity Section was to gain the acceptance by the whole Assembly, for study in the member churches subsequently, of an attempt to put into words a picture of the unity we seek. The statement is as follows.

**"We believe that the unity which is both God's**

[1] The authors in the present series were all asked to read John Lawrence's book *The Hard Facts of Unity* (S.C.M., 1961) and to use it as a common point of reference.

**will and His gift to His Church is being made visible as all in each place who are baptized into Jesus Christ and confess Him as Lord and Saviour are brought by the Holy Spirit into one fully committed fellowship, holding the one apostolic faith, preaching the one Gospel, breaking the one bread, joining in common prayer, and having a corporate life reaching out in witness and service to all and who at the same time are united with the whole Christian fellowship in all places and all ages in such-wise that ministry and members are accepted by all, and that all can act and speak together as occasion requires for the tasks to which God calls His people."**

It has taken forty years of ecumenical converse to reach that point. Yet when the statement is analysed,[1] it quickly reveals how much still remains to be done before there is even agreement on the nature of our goal, let alone before it is reached.

But the conversation goes on. This series is intended to be another modest contribution to it. Humanly speaking, the goal of Christian unity is ludicrously impracticable. But God never commands the impossible. We believe that unity is His command, and that in our time He is giving to us the encouragement of seeing things happen which our fathers would have considered impossible. It is in that faith that these contributions are offered. God is leaving us in no doubt that the world which He has made is ineluctably *one* world. Within it, at the place where reconciliation is proclaimed, we must not be divided.

✠ OLIVER BRISTOL

[1] See the *Official Report*, page 116, published by S.C.M. Press.

## AUTHOR'S PREFACE

I AM obliged to state, beyond possibility of misunderstanding, that the following pages express the personal statement of a Congregationalist, and not any official view of the Congregational Union. I understand that the publishers of this series of books have sought such personal, rather than official, statements, and I accepted the honour of being asked to write this one because, holding no office in any Congregational Union apart from that of the ministry, I felt free to say what is here said, and to say it largely in the first person singular. I shall, of course, be sorry if what I say gives offence, or is thought grossly unfair, by any of my own communion. I would not deliberately offend any, or ignore the view of any. However that may turn out to be, let nobody outside Congregationalism think of the views here expressed as views for which Congregationalism as a whole may be held to account.

Secondly, I have to say that I write here with knowledge of only two of the Congregational Unions that exist in the world—those of England and Wales, and of Scotland. Australia, South Africa and Welsh-speaking Wales have Congregational Unions of which I know nothing, and whose ecumenical views may, for all I know, be as the poles apart from what I here assume.

I have not thought it necessary here to say more than a very little about our history. It happens that during the present year two books on this subject have appeared: a large and learned one by Professor Tudur Jones, *Congrega-*

*tionalism in England*, and my own much slighter volume, *The Story of Congregationalism*. Dr. Harry Escott published in 1960 *The History of Congregationalism in Scotland*, which again is a fully documented and extensive work. Reference to these will provide what the reader requires if he wishes to learn more of our historical background. Details of these will be found in the Bibliography at the end of the present book.

This will express the assumptions and the limitations of the present undertaking.

We are feeling our way. More than that we cannot yet say.

ERIK ROUTLEY

EDINBURGH
May, 1962

# CONTENTS

# 1

# Elusive Unity

## Images of Unity

ANYONE who has done much reading and pondering knows that words have many strange properties. One of these is that if you look at a single word for long enough, isolating it from any context or syntax, it begins to look odd; before your eyes it disintegrates, losing its meaning altogether, and becoming a strange shape or sound, which looks stranger—because more meaningless—the more you stare at it. There is another parallel quality in words which are, for any reason, constantly used in imperative contexts, and constantly heard by people whom the users of the words wish to direct or improve. In such a case, the word becomes first a slogan—a half-significant yet emotive sound—and then an irritant that makes the sensitive hearer say, "Let me hear that once more and I shall scream."

"Unity," in the Christian sense, is now such a word. Nobody ought now to use it without doing what he can to restore to it some of that historic meaning which in popular and official over-use it has largely lost.

When we speak of "unity" nowadays, we must not be unaware that any of the following images will present themselves to our hearers' minds: and that it is as likely as not that the very images we would rather suppress are those of which our hearers are most conscious.

Consider some of these images, and consider their diversity and elusiveness.

Unity can mean that unity in Christ which is possessed by the whole company of Christians in virtue of their acknowledgement that Christ is their Head and Redeemer. This unity is an inseparable property of the whole invisible Church (that is, the Church whose numbers are known only to God); it cannot be separated from this great company; it is never in question; it can never be the subject of exhortation; it is the one thing which all Christians necessarily have in common.

Unity can also mean a visible unity of opinion and doctrine which is evident not only to Christians but also to unbelievers: in virtue of this unity the Church can be said to "speak with one voice," to "present an undivided front." This unity is a function of expediency in times and places where the Church's authority is not taken for granted. Its opposite is seen primarily in such situations as the disagreement between one large body of Christians and all the rest on the ethics of birth-control or the authority of the Pope. But it is also seen in trans-denominational planes when Christians disagree publicly, and therefore fail to provide a "lead" on such an issue as the use of nuclear weapons or the use of alcoholic drink.

Unity can, therefore, mean to many people a unanimity of view which many feel to be unnatural and therefore improperly urged by unity's apostles. Unity, in the minds of such objectors, ultimately spells totalitarian dictatorship with the suppression of minority views and a forced identity of public speech. The opposite of this unity, say such objectors, is freedom such as man is entitled to demand at his neighbour's and his superior's hands, and such as the powerful are always planning to wrest from him.

Unity can again mean uniformity of public practice: uniformity in church government which suppresses all but (one supposes) one of the existing forms of church government; uniformity of worship which suppresses all but one of the existing patterns of liturgy. Objectors to the first uniformity bring political consciences in evidence; objectors to the second, aesthetic and customary arguments. At this level, much doctrine is disputed and much law quoted.

Or unity can present itself as an invasion of privacy and even property: certainly an invasion of vested interests. Unity may demand the closing of cherished buildings, the merging of congregations, the cultivation of new friendships, the learning of new hymns, the severing of long-established ties. Its opposite is the continuing comfort of the local congregation and the familiar appurtenances of worship—a comfort whose cultivation nobody has the right to call merely sinful.

To yet others, unity presents itself as an absolute necessity for mission and evangelism. How, say they, can we speak in the name of Christ to the heathen in this or any other country when we are divided, and when we cannot but appear to be making competing claims on the personal allegiance of those to whom we speak? Some believe—we can subsume this under this main heading—that the overt disunity of the churches is one of the most pernicious impediments to faith in the unbeliever who is at our own gates; this I personally believe to be much exaggerated, in that it is more often an excuse for avoiding the necessity of responsible decision than a genuine complaint against the churches' behaviour when a man produces our disunity as a reason for his unfaithfulness. Not always, but very often, there is another reason, less comfortably to be expressed and admitted, shielded behind this stock response to our disunity. That apart, however, it is very evident that the Church of South India has come into being primarily because of the conviction that a united church is a better evangelizing instrument than an aggregation of divided communions.

To others, unity is strength, unity is power. . . .

And to the Gospel, unity is none of these things. It is what Cyprian said it was. It is charity.

## The Counterpoint of Charity

I wish at the outset to declare a personal conviction which I believe to be far from irrelevant to the present assignment. There is, as I believe, one situation in which, above all others, men are men, and at their best: in which they have felicity of a settled and yet vivid kind that is comparable to that which we ascribe to heaven. It is a situation from which no man is by nature excluded by any defect of wealth or rank, by any accident of birth whatever except, perhaps, that of mental deficiency or derangement. It is, on the other hand, a situation from which the accidents of human life cut off many, and from which many others cut off themselves. This is the situation of *lively conversation*. There are times when a man knows this felicity, when he is in the company of a friend, or of several friends; when every man's possessions of mind and spirit are fully shared; when nobody keeps back part of the price; when there is none of the conventional fear or suspicion or guardedness which cause reserve and hypocrisy in human encounter; when every man is very fully "himself," and very fully at the disposal of all the others. This is when conversation sparkles, or when silence is eloquently companionable. This is something which anybody enjoys; indeed, it is perhaps the most simple, as well as the most exquisite, pleasure known to men. It is what is common to absolutely all men, and what distinguishes all men from the beasts. Children know it—the pure joy of being with another—just being, the conversation, if there be any, being an expression of the *being together*. Much so-called "civilized" life is a conspiracy to estrange men and women from this situation; to place comfortable barriers between them so that the demands of this vivacious joy, with their possible embarrassments, may not be too clamorous: the consequence is always the withdrawal of the joy and the dehumanizing of the people. That this is the true essence of marriage who happily married would want to deny? That it is the focus of friendship, who does not really know? And that this was the dynamic of the primitive Church is the very evident testimony of the early chapters of the Acts of the Apostles.

I personally do not believe that I am interested in any other kind of pleasure; I do not believe that I fear anything quite so much as the dilution or destruction of the relation which I know is possible between me and other men; and I am vexed and made miserable by nothing so much as the dreary necessities which common life presents of being, in the presence of others, half a man or a quarter of a man because of some convention of social intercourse, or some known suspicion or touchiness in the air, or of some social activity calculated to keep me at a distance from my neighbour so that everybody can achieve a formal but never indecorous affability.

To present the unity of the apostolic Church in terms of "communism" is obviously to miss the central point, and to mislead one's hearers. Communism is by definition an obligatory and impersonal sharing. The heart of the primitive Church was the pleasure that the apostles took in one another's company and one another's gifts. This pleasure was the direct gift of the Holy Spirit: they knew a fresh kind of "oneness" from the moment of Pentecost. And they called this *agape*, charity.

It is against the breach of this that St. Paul offers all his doctrine of church unity. In 1 Corinthians 12 to 14, that classic triptych, he writes first of the danger that lies in the denial by one person or party of his need of the other, then of the great glory of charity, and finally of the danger of being esoteric and denying the communion of the mind. In his eleventh chapter, the profanation of the Lord's Table lies in the kind of contemptuous and thoughtless behaviour between members of the Church which poisons communication and frustrates true encounter; in the second chapter of Philippians his exalted passage on the humiliation and glorification of Christ is ushered in by an exhortation that men shall admit and express their need of one another in the Church, and not "look only on their own matters."

Joy in one another and joy in the Lord go together in the primitive doctrine of the Church. Love of the brethren and love of the Lord are indivorcible in the eyes of the author of 1 St. John.

> As Thou dost join with holiest bonds
> The Father and the Son,
> So fill Thy saints with mutual love
> And link their hearts in one.

This is what I shall show to be the heart of Congregationalist doctrine celebrated in a hymn which as a matter of fact Congregationalists never sing. But this doctrine of the "love of the brethren," of what Mr. John Wren Lewis is in our own time calling "The God between us," is exactly what moved the earliest Congregationalists to engage in their peculiar, and oddly truculent, form of Dissent.

But this is to anticipate. I am still for the moment speaking generally—and yet also personally. I believe that when Cyprian urged his contemporaries to recall the Unity of the Church (in his *De Unitate*) it was to charity—the charity which they had broken by their insulting and frivolous reaction to the schism and its causes—more than to doctrinal conformity—which the schismatics had broken—that he was calling his hearers. It is at this level alone that one can speak penetratingly about unity. At other levels one can speak officially, and secondarily, and in a manner which emergency may make necessary. But the problem that faces the Church of the present day is basically the ancient, natural problem of encounter: the recovery of the joy of encounter: the recall of Christians to a courage that will face the demands of that joy (so light an affliction will earn so great a prize!): and the repudiation of all speech, all behaviour, all habit of thought that presumes to disparage that joy. If men within the church—the local church—can show the pattern of this joy, communions of Christians will seek to have this joy with one another; and that which exists between men at their best will exist between groups, between communions, between national groups and catholic communions.

The stage at which we now stand is surely not the ultimate stage. It would be presumptuous to believe that the will of

B

God will be finally achieved in our own time. The vision of a universal charity, a universal encounter, is a remote one; and it ought to be remote. It is much remoter than the vision of a single organized church controlled by a single international body. Being remoter, it is probably truer. Being more natural, more directly connected with what all rational beings already know, it is the more surely truer.

But at our present stage there is one aspect of this unity which we must not overlook. Charity suffers long and is kind: but charity is not the negation of personality. Encounter is not achieved when this person entirely dominates that person; when the "Yes" and "No" of the second party are called forth merely by a desire to please, or a fear of offending, the first. The kind of encounter between persons of which I was thinking when I first mentioned it is an encounter between real persons, a costly and, between sinners, always hazardous relation. At its centre is the courage of being, not the more comfortable yieldingness of non-being. In crude terms at the ecumenical level nobody will be excited for very long about uniting with a body that turns out not to be there at all.

The ecumenical Church of which our prophets dream, and of which our young men see visions, ought to be more like sixteenth-century counterpoint than seventeenth-century opera. An equality of excellences (to use a phrase which the recent work of Daniel Jenkins suggests) is the true pattern. Those who know what sixteenth-century counterpoint really consists of will realize that the difference between it and eighteenth-century opera is not so much that the opera presents a tune in one voice to which all the others are subordinated in accompaniment, while the polyphony presents a consort of equal voices; but rather that in itself the polyphony is a texture built up partly of harmonious interplay of equal parts, and partly of momentarily prominent "leads" where this or that voice makes a statement which the others follow and comment on. So in the Church we look not for the domination of what we now think of as one "party" or "denomination" or "ethos," all the other sheaves bowing down to Joseph's sheaf; but yet neither for a levelled-down equality where none is permitted any distinction; rather we seek a texture of vital voices, the "lead," the prophecy, the invention in the Holy Spirit, coming now from here, now from there, all being alert for the moment when, on the statement of such a "lead," the pattern changes, while the music continues uninterrupted.

I want now to show, as I believe that without any special pleading I can, that there is that in Congregationalism which on the one hand respects and indeed calls to the attention of all of us the texture, while on the other it has historically announced a "lead" which the other parties to the pattern ought not to ignore—and indeed have been unable to ignore. We can see this all the better if we all admit that historically Congregationalism has fallen into all manner of error, such as has spoiled the pattern and made it in certain generations very difficult indeed to trace. But this curious church polity, which began in a situation of radical and furious dissent, and than which none showed at its inception less promise of being anything but an enemy of unity, has something to say which with due respect its holders wish others to hear. What it has to say concerns the "love of the brethren" and the unity that is charity.

# 2

# Traditional Dissent

## "Avoid congregationalism"

BISHOP Hensley Henson once wrote to a junior priest of his own church, "Avoid congregationalism like the plague." He, a man of delicate and precise habits in writing, spelt the word with a small "c"; and by this he meant, "avoid what people please to call democratic patterns in church life: they never work." Provided that everybody understands that historically Congregationalism has virtually nothing to do with democracy, the Congregationalists will have some chance of being understood by their Christian brothers.

It may well be true that the Puritan respect for the rights of the intelligent man (I detect very little in Puritan teaching about the rights of the unintelligent, the shiftless or the negligent) proved to be a sound foundation for modern democratic practices in politics. But if democracy is government by representation and decision by majority vote, this never had any place in the teaching of historic Congregationalists. It is much truer to say that the first Congregationalists were anarchists than to say that they were democrats. But it is fairer to accept that they thought of themselves as the apostles of government through friendship.

The history of Congregationalism can be read elsewhere. This is not the place to recount it. It will be familiar to most readers of these pages, anyhow, that this form of radical Dissent had its origin in the teachings of Robert Browne (*c.* 1550–1633), who for a decade or so (1580–90) pursued certain adventures in local church government, and set down his principles in writing. There had been schisms of an Anabaptist, Lollard and catharist sort as long as there had been church history. The uniqueness of Robert Browne's adventure was not in its puritanism—its separating itself from the world of unbelievers, half-believers, conformist Christians and all who were not evidently and professedly of the true elect—but rather in the systematic manner in which its leaders found it possible to argue their case in church politics. True, this Dissent against the Elizabethan Settlement had its very positive Anabaptist side: a very close adherence to the letter of Scripture, a hatred of ceremony and symbolism, a suspicion of all that we now call Establishment, and a special suspicion of episcopacy. There was more than a touch of temperamental nonconformity, even temperamental disobedience, about Brownism. But these things it shared with all manner of schismatic sects in previous history. None of these sects produced a literature like the writings of Browne and Henry Barrow and Thomas Greenwood. Between them (and they did not by any means agree with one another at every point) these produced a reasoned doctrine of the Church which was based on what Browne himself called "the communion of graces." More logical and less compromising than the Presbyterian Dissenters (such as Thomas Cartwright), these men claimed in effect that they were only interested in two kinds of "church"—the universal company of believers and the local embodiment of that company. All attempts by others to "organize" the local churches into groups they repudiated. Where the Presbyterians were for substituting a system of "classes" for the Anglican system of dioceses—seeking by their reform to found a church order which should be free of state-association and purified of corruption, but not wholly free of delegated human authority—the Brownists would sweep away all ecumenical organization whatever. Their concern, eloquently argued, was for the purity of the local congregation; and if they had any view of an ecumenical church, it was that ecumenicity—in any visible sense—must bring with it impurity.

### Four Ancient Causes of Separation

By way of direct evidence, consider the Four Causes of Separation which Henry Barrow[1] mentions in his tract of that title (1587). They are: (1) That the Anglican churches worship the true God in a false manner; (2) that their principle of church membership, based on geographical rather than directly spiritual qualifications, is unacceptable; (3) that the ministry of the Church of England is inadequately qualified, irresponsibly selected, and improperly supported by tithes and endowments; and (4) that the control of the Church by an episcopate carrying an authority partly secular (in that it is bound up with the authority of parliament and makes possible "spiritual courts") is repellent. This is a typical formulation of the Brownist Dissent, taken from the most prolific of Brownist writers. The objection to Presbyterianism was, of course, that it was not radical enough in its reformation of church order. Any reply that such a compromise as Presbyterianism of the sixteenth-

[1] *c.* 1550–93. One of several Brownists executed in 1593 for sedition.

century pattern might provide would leave room for an ecumenical development in the Church the Brownists would, with one mind, have dismissed as irrelevant.

I do not believe that we are here required to rehearse history. What is necessary now is to ask—how much of all this is relevant at present? Upon what ground now do Congregationalists continue in Dissent?

Has this anything in common with the ground that Barrow took? The answer is—very little. What has happened now to his four reasons for separation?

(1) *Worship*

In worship, Congregationalists no longer refer to the Book of Common Prayer as "a piece of swine's flesh," or "Dagon's stump." Indeed, they not only admire it as religious literature but not infrequently use parts of it, even large parts of it, in their own worship. When they do not do this, they publish and use directories and prayer-books of their own devising. True, in most of Congregationalism there are at least two points at which their view of the Prayer Book cannot be regarded by Anglicans as a satisfactory one. On the one hand, Congregationalists still cherish what we call "freedom of worship," and while they no longer disparage the prayer-book as such, they would find intolerable any legal obligation to use it and it only, no less than their fathers did. On the other hand, no Anglican lover of the prayer-book as a vehicle of liturgy is particularly impressed by the disconnected raptures with which a Dissenter can often now be heard to say that, of course, the Prayer Book is incomparable literature. The book was not designed to be an aesthetic monument, and whether one finds it beautiful, and enjoys the occasional Cathedral

Evensong on a summer Saturday afternoon, is quite beside the point of ecumenical encounter.

(2) *The Parish*

Barrow's second objection has retained more of its weight. Congregationalists still reject the "parish system"—although to be sure a good deal of the emphasis with which they reject it comes from the necessity of having to make the best of having no parish system. Two communions cannot have a parish system, and the system is part of the communion from which Congregationalists are in dissent. Therefore their congregations are still drawn from a wide area, and consist (as do those of all non-Anglican churches) of all those of like mind who live within travelling distance of the church, not of all baptized Christians within a stated region. But the distinction thus implied is in fact breaking down at many points. Why, for example, when a certain area in a new housing estate happens to be served, or apparently served, by a Congregational church, do the locals often call the Congregational minister "Vicar," and expect him, as part of the general social services of the community, to baptize their children and conduct their weddings? Why (moreover) do such people receive a great surprise if such a minister begins, on being asked for such a service, to speak in strong terms of church membership? The answer is not merely because the people are ignorant, because "all churches are the same to them now." That is so, but it is not the basic reason for such a manifestation of what might be called passive ecumenism. Part of the reason—and I believe the more important part—is that the Congregational minister now takes few steps publicly to separate himself from the activity of the church in general. In dress he is indistinguishable from his anglican neighbour, as he is now in education and social habits. He is poorer, but nobody in the council-houses knows that. He is looked upon as part of "the church in general" because for a good deal of the time he behaves as though he were a minister of "the church in general." He may not be responsible for the parish in the sense of saying "All these souls are mine," but the difference between him and the true parish priest is now a difference of which the half-heathen estate-dweller knows nothing at all.

This is, of course, the consequence of the evangelical revival. The idea of the strictly "gathered" church, intent on achieving a high standard of purity, and subordinating all missionary work to that, broke down spectacularly under the impact of the evangelical revival. If there were a true Brownist now among Congregational ministers, he would take a very different line on the housing estate from what the present-day minister takes, and is required by his colleagues to take. Such a Brownist would be more likely to gather, after diligent searching, six covenanted Christians in the front room of his manse every Sabbath morning for catechizing, preaching and the breaking of bread, than to devote all his energies to filling, or half-filling, the attractive modern two-hundred-seating building with adjacent halls which is now known as his church. Further comment on this situation must wait a moment, but we will give it. The point at the moment is that if Congregationalists reject the parish-system to-day, it is for reasons very different from those for which Barrow rejected it, and in a surrounding situation very different from his.

(3) *The Ministry*

As to the selection, and the maintenance of the Anglican ministry, a modern Congregationalist would know—or ought to know—what vast changes have come since the time of Barrow: on the one hand, in the methods of selection of candidates for the priesthood (some of the most significant of these, we understand, have taken place since the Second World War), and on the other, in the economic situation which has seen to it that the clergy are no longer to be assumed to be wealthy or even comfortably-off; and therefore that touch of "superior poverty" which undoubtedly was not absent from Barrow's strictures on the Anglican system, and equally that association of the clergy with a landed class to which, as a matter of sociology, Dissenters tended not to belong, has disappeared. Free Churchmen do not now attend much to the superior economics of Anglicans: and what is more, a fusion of social classes makes it easier for an Anglican and a Free Churchman to speak together. True—the Establishment is still officially disapproved by all Free Churchmen; but it is far less a matter of open and acrimonious dispute than it was even fifty years ago. The maintenance of the Anglican ministry is a by-product of the Establishment, and Congregationalists might still be disposed to prefer that ministers be supported by their own people than from those sources which remain mysterious to those who are not in the inner Anglican counsels: but they would be dishonest if they denied that this has raised economic difficulties in these later days so serious as to provide a major threat to their continuance as a separate denomination. (See below, pp. 67–70.)

(4) *Episcopacy*

Perhaps it is Barrow's fourth point of dissent that is to-day the most lively one among Free Churchmen in general and Congregationalists especially. Episcopacy is, as everybody knows, one of the most vexatious points of disagreement between the communions. In the traditional Congregationalist dissent, as we know it to-day, there is still something of the Brownist touch. To Barrow, episcopacy meant (*a*) power, which he believed to be a corrupting force in general, and (*b*) a connection with the State, which he believed to be a corrupting force especially at that time. Turning back to his New Testament, Barrow, in common with all of like mind, claimed that a bishop is a minister—neither more nor less. With the Ignatian settlement or the Cyprianic development of the episcopate he would have nothing to do—still less with later expansions of episcopacy. That one man should be in any kind of authority over a true minister of the Word was to such as Barrow repellent because this authority would obscure the direct authority which through His ministry Christ exercised over the gathered congregation. The minister was the only person who could be regarded in any sense as an intermediary of Christ's authority, and this sense was for the Brownist a carefully restricted one.

As to the State—the Lollard and Anabaptist traditions contained a decisive protest against any connection between the Church and the State. The State, to such, was an unclean thing; civic office was often explicitly forbidden to Christians of these persuasions. That the sovereign should be the titular head of the Church was an outrage to such a conscience, and the political nexus between crown and see in their sight irrevocably tainted the episcopate.

The history of England and of Europe in those times—a history which continued for a long time in the same key—was such as to encourage this kind of dissent against episcopacy. Bishops and archbishops were indeed politicians of decisive influence, and politics was then no cleaner a game than it is now. Sensitive consciences might well find it difficult to reconcile the Christian calling with influential participation in high diplomacy. On the other hand, there developed among the Puritan sections of the English Church a very strong sense of the necessity that the righteousness of God should be enthroned in public life: but the traditional doubt of the propriety of ministerial participation in politics produced a lively sense of lay participation which came to its highest manifestation in Cromwell. At a later stage, Dissenters turned out to be the kind of people who were much sought after for public office, especially at the local level; and the ironic turn of history which caused Dissenters to be precluded by statute from public office (so that if a Dissenter were called on, for example, to be Lord Mayor of London, he must become a formal communicant of the Church of England before he was eligible—a situation which prevailed from the days of the Clarendon Code until the early nineteenth century) was enough to keep alive a sense among Dissenters that it was not only their duty but their right to engage in politics.

But this was—or appeared to them to be—a different matter from the acceptance of an episcopacy which belonged to the Establishment. In any case Dissenters as politicians had little patience with the Establishment. One point must, however, be added here concerning the Brownist objection to episcopacy; it is a negative one, but none the less important.

It is that a true Brownist would have been incapable of seeing what defenders of episcopacy regard as its ecumenical value. It is historically true that the expansion of *episkope* from the connotation of local ministry to that of regional ministry was the consequence of a natural need in scattered churches to have a visible principle of unity; if there was a person to whom they could look as an impersonation of their unity and common cause with their brothers in other places, this gave them a needed sense of security and solidarity. That was the point of the Ignatian Settlement. It may not be a New Testament doctrine, but it is a natural and, as many believe, a wholly blameless development. Such a point would not occur to a Brownist. He was too clearly conscious of the corruptions of "unity": of the abuses of prelacy: of the improper extensions of papal or episcopal power. The sight of a bishop meant to him not ground for thoughts of unity but ground for thoughts of schism. History and his conscience forbade him even to consider this point.

History has moved, and consciences have to some extent softened. Therefore to-day in Congregationalism there is a system of ecumenical ministry whose inception in 1919 was an admission that not everything that had been said against episcopacy in 1589 remained relevant. The Moderators of the Congregational Union of England and Wales (the office does not exist in other Congregational Unions) were appointed to exercise an ecumenical ministry: to keep the churches of their regions in touch with one another: to act as "Fathers in God" to the ministers of their regions: to give advice in matters of discipline, strategy and church extension. It is interesting to observe how, once the system of Moderators had been established, a touch of "episcopal" ethos soon added itself to their status. In particular it may be said that nowadays (1962) it is very rare for an ordination to be carried out in the Congregational Union of England and Wales without the presence of the Moderator. It is not held that a Moderator is indispensable to an ordination, as in Anglican circles it is held that a bishop is indispensable. But it is only a minority who feel it fitting that the Moderator should not be invited to an ordination in his province.

Moderatorial power is still strictly circumscribed. The old puritan tag that all power in ordained persons is "ministerial, not magisterial" applies very much to moderators. They are backed by no church courts, they are not in any sense lawgivers. Such influence as they may exert is very largely the consequence of careful application of their personal gifts. But with those large limitations, their appointment was a withdrawal from any total dissent from episcopacy. It could be argued by any who wished to disparage the Dissenting way that the moderators are in an almost impossible position: that a large organization of churches cannot be administered by people who have no authority that is not strictly spiritual: that the nine provinces of this Congregational Union, each with its moderator, are all too large to be administered with the spiritual efficiency that can be achieved in an English diocese: that the Moderator, having charge of so enormous an area as that, for example, which includes Shrewsbury and Reading, or another which includes Chester and Hertford, must inevitably be in greater danger of becoming a "travelling V.I.P." than is an Anglican bishop. Justice would demand a certain modification of such propositions; it is particularly necessary to remember that faithfulness is not extinguished by any difficulty of situation. In the Moderators' case, it is not.

But what we are here noting is simply that the institution of Moderators was an ecumenical act—indeed, an act more ecumenical in its consequences than its original proposers may have known.

# 3

# Continuing Convictions

WE have already stated some of the properties of modern Congregationalism in this examination of the relevance of one brief historic document. I wish now to add a more positive statement of continuing Congregational belief. I shall make the statement now: its implications and the dangers to which it exposes us in any encounter with other communions will, I think, be sufficiently explained and admitted as we go on. But my statement is this: that throughout its history Congregationalism has adhered to the principle of church government by friendship.

## Church Meeting

In a Congregational church the governing principle (humanly speaking) is the Church Meeting. It is, say Congregationalists, through the Church Meeting that Christ rules in His Church, and "church" is classically assumed to be equivalent to "local church." The church meeting is composed of all the "members" of the church. None is excluded, and none has more power than another. A "member" is he or she who, having been baptized and instructed in the Faith, has openly and personally made covenant with the Church, confessing the Faith and promising to keep the peace of the Church, and who on making such covenant has been received into full membership. This principle of personal covenant, though in the outward form of its making it has changed and in many places corrupted itself, has never been absent from the Congregationalist doctrine of churchmanship.

In practice this means that all decisions that pertain to the local church are taken by the whole body of believers in that place. The distinguishing quality about "church meeting" is that it is an act of the church which in practice only approximates to a certain ideal; it is not an act which is based on a legal foundation prescribing the minimum that may be achieved in the hope that in favourable circumstances more may be achieved. It is rather an act which is never perfect, but which is carried out in the conviction that the pattern to which it approximates is the will of the Lord.

This pattern is that according to which every member present has equal right and duty to contribute to the discussion of a matter before the meeting, and equal responsibility for the decision finally taken. Ideally, at least on matters of primary spiritual importance, a decision is not taken until all are agreed that it is in conformity with the will of God. Therefore matters are not decided by vote; rather, the proposal is modified again and again in the light of the accumulating wisdom of the members, so that in the end it reaches a conclusion of which each may say "This is right, and nearer to the will of God than that which by myself I should have decided."

In the working out of this technique, certain gifts are presupposed in the members. If it can be shown that these gifts are such as any Christian ought to strive for, and such as can be expected of any Christian irrespective of his worldly status, the doctrine is a respectable one. We believe that this is in fact so. It is necessary that all members shall to some extent have the gift of conversation—being able to express themselves, and to listen to and be corrected by the views that others express. It is assumed that each will have something to contribute—not to every discussion separately, but to the total wisdom expressed in all the meeting's deliberations; this in turn presupposes that each will *be a person*, and permit others to be themselves, in Church Meeting. It is implied by this (although so to state it is to use language foreign to puritan theology) that to be covenanted with Christ and with one's fellow-members is to realize oneself as a person. It is further assumed that no decision before a Church Meeting will be of such a sort that delay through the necessity of reconciling disagreements will have worse consequences than the hurrying of a decision without regard to a dissenting minority.

All this is an interpretation of Church Meeting with which, I suspect, Congregationalists would find it easy to agree; but it will not be found so written in any single document of Congregational history. It is the way in which Church Meeting has developed from the days of Browne to our own, and we may especially note how much it owes to the practice of the Quakers (whose technique of worship and church order itself developed slowly, beginning, but only beginning, with George Fox's demonstration of 1656).

What it all fundamentally implies is that the members of the church shall be in charity with one another: which means in modern language that they shall enjoy one another's company, be alert to one another's wisdom, and be unwilling to find fault with one another: where such attitudes are not directly attainable through the inclinations of grace, it is assumed that they will be cultivated as a duty of courtesy.

### Modern Modifications

It will be evident that this high doctrine has always in practice to suffer certain modifications, and is liable to certain corruptions.

1. The greatly increased mobility of ordinary people in our day as compared with the seventeenth century makes much more difficult that close nexus of mutual regard, and therefore that candour of disposition, which in ancient days made the Church Meeting so august an instrument of the divine guidance.

2. The greatly increased size of Congregational churches—with which has naturally gone a dilution of membership-qualifications—is liable to produce a Church Meeting which is too unwieldy to reach a corporate decision otherwise than through the guidance of a few, and many of whose members lack the sense of responsibility which would make them ready to make an effective contribution. In consequence the larger the membership, the smaller the number of people whose influence in the government of the church is decisive. Indeed, this has led to the abandonment of Church Meeting altogether in certain communions which call themselves Congregational—notably in America, where the physical expansion of congregations has been most marked.

3. Evangelical doctrine, which has insisted more firmly on placing men and women in a position where they may receive salvation than on examining in the Calvinist style their qualifications for membership, has contributed to the

dilution of membership-privilege, and to the large size of some congregations. This has a similar effect on Church Meeting.

4. While congregations meeting in Congregational churches have always been to some extent geographically scattered—the churches are known paradoxically as "gathered churches," but the phrase means gathered from a scattered area—they are now much more so; less even than formerly—much less—do the diverse members of a modern Congregational church meet one another in the communities where they live.

All this has led to the adoption by most Church Meetings of a pattern now familiar, but lacking the fullness of the original conception. It has always been a principle in Congregationalism that the church should be "ruled" by Elders: "ruled" meaning, of course, guided rather than legally directed.[1] Of the Elders the minister traditionally is one; and among the body of Elders are (in the doctrine of John Owen, Congregationalism's leading theological mind in the mid-seventeenth century) "ruling" and "teaching" elders, the minister being of the former kind. The "rule" of the church is its spiritual direction, and the doctrine of Church Meeting has never excluded the obvious necessity for a small body of experienced and sanctified persons who in matters of discipline or in matters where some clear directive may properly be required from the most experienced, will do their duty in the name of the whole church. Nowadays these Elders are called Deacons; but their function nowadays has less that is disciplinary and more that is prudential. In former days much attention was paid to the

[1] The classic document for Congregational Church Order is John Owen's *The True Nature of a Gospel-Church* (1655).

examination of candidates for membership, and the scrutiny of the lives of members in case there might be any whose behaviour made it necessary to separate them from the membership. In practice these functions are now rarely exercised by deacons. On the other hand, in many churches deacons pay regular pastoral visits to the congregation by districts, and in all cases deacons meet regularly to discuss with the minister the church's strategy. What can become an abuse, however, is the assumption by the diaconate of work that belongs properly to a Church Meeting, and the constant depression of Church Meeting into an instrument for formally ratifying a series of diaconal decisions. In very large churches the problem is acute, and in some cases has been solved by the appointment of a Church Council—a deliberative and executive body with prudential powers of the widest sort.

Another pattern which forms itself in large congregations very commonly is for the Church Meeting to consist in practice of some forty or fifty people who attend the monthly meeting and act in the name of the Church. They become an unofficial Church Council. There may be 400 members on the roll, but the other 350 contentedly accept what the fifty have decided.

Honesty obliges us, of course, to admit that surely in very few cases even in the most classic days can Church Meeting have consisted of a hundred per cent of the membership. It is now tacitly admitted that if every family in the church is represented by one person at Church Meeting, the meeting is doing as well as it can be hoped to do. In what circumstances can two parents with young children go out together to Church Meeting on a Wednesday night? Only (*a*) if the family is united enough to have a grandparent living in the house, or an unmarried aunt or some such relative, (*b*) if a child-sitter can be organized, or (*c*) if affluence extends to a resident servant. Condition (*a*) has disappeared through social mobility; condition (*c*) cannot by definition be a condition of church membership. Condition (*b*) may be achieved by good fortune but cannot be depended on, and likewise cannot be regarded as a condition of full membership.

The truth, of course, is that Congregationalism inherits its classic traditions from a time when the place of women in church life was almost entirely ignored. A Church Meeting consisting of the men of the congregation would in Puritan days have been regarded as a full meeting. If women attended (there is no evidence that they never did, although it is highly improbable that they were in those days admitted to eldership) no doubt they were tolerated; but their absence would not be thought of as a serious impediment to the right working of the Meeting.

And yet—with all these qualifications and all these difficulties, Congregationalists will still insist that Church Meeting *works*; that there is such a thing as government by friendship. And they would be on safe ground if they ventured a little further. It is common knowledge that other communions are not without organizations that look like church meetings. Especially in recent years, the rise of the parish or congregational meeting in the Church of England—the very development which caused Bishop Henson to utter his warning about congregationalism—has answered an evident need for a less hierarchical system of government in that church. Those Anglicans who approve this movement towards greater lay participation in church government must forgive the Congregationalists if they say that Church Meeting did not primarily arise in response to a demand for democratic government in the Church. Nothing could have been further from the mind of Browne and Barrow and Owen. Browne was about as undemocratic, impatient, and intolerant a person as ever appeared even in that period of church history. Such men are men of conviction: and Browne saw Church Meeting in terms of the "communion of graces," the interaction of persons, the counterpoint of authorities, which is something very different from making concessions to those who look for the wider distribution of responsibility.[1]

To all this we shall have to return: but this central conviction of Congregationalists is one which, however obscurely it is held in some quarters, Congregationalists would be unwilling to allow to disappear from the church at large. What part its fruits might play in a united church I shall at a later stage suggest.

[1] For a modern official statement, in an ecumenical context, of the Congregationalist convictions about Church Meeting, see the Appendix, page 92.

# 4

# Present Customs

IF Congregationalists are invited to look at proposals for the union of the churches, they are not only liable, they are positively obliged, to consider two questions: what the united church might stand to gain by their being incorporated within it, and what they would stand to lose by the disappearance of their separate organization.

I have already said something of the doctrine of the Church Meeting, as a distinctively Congregationalist doctrine.[1] I have hinted also at certain implications of the fact that this is an ideal doctrine, not a legal one. The most important of these implications remains to be stated: it is that, being a doctrine which can best be put into practice in small groups, and which tends to prove impracticable in the large groups which Congregationalists have formed during the past four or five generations, it is a doctrine singularly suited for incorporation in a united church. Paradoxical though this might sound, it is surely the truth; but it is best

[1] It ought to be made plain that Baptists hold the doctrine of the Church Meeting, and in church order are indistinguishable from Congregationalists, having "superintendents" where Congregationalists now have moderators. In church order they are Congregational: their point of divergence is solely on the doctrine of believers' baptism.

explained if we consider in what sense Congregationalists have now the right to call themselves a distinctive Christian body. In brief—can Congregationalists call themselves "a church"?

I am about to state a view which, as I believe, is not wholly in accord with the official view of the Congregational Union of England and Wales. (As I write, I am a member of the Congregational Union of Scotland.)

### "Church" or "Churches"?

Traditionally, Protestants of the kind of which Congregationalism is an example have held a certain view of the use of the word "church." They have tended to use it in two senses, and only these two: first, the whole company of Christian believers, and second, the local community gathered in worship and in Church Meeting. Thus they will speak of "the church" as the church universal (whose precise extent is known only to God), and they will speak of "the church" at Richmond Hill, Bournemouth, or at Chorlton Road, Manchester. Another division, which gives even greater precision, prevailed in the days when the *building* was referred to not as a church but as a chapel, or, earlier, a meeting-house. A Congregational preacher can still say, and say significantly, to his people: "*this* in which we meet is the chapel: *you* are the church."

But Congregationalists have not, until very recently, countenanced the expression "The Congregational Church," meaning the whole company of Congregationalists. The organized body of Congregational churches has always been referred to as a Congregational Union: and there exist to-day Congregational Unions of England and Wales, of Scotland, of Ireland, of Wales (known as the "Union of

Welsh Independents"), of Australia, of New Zealand, and of South Africa. Congregationalism does not now exist separately in the United States or in Canada. Churches approximating to the Congregational way are to be found in many other countries, such as Germany, Holland, and Sweden in Europe, and here and there in Latin America: that these do not refer to themselves as "Unions," but use such titles as "The Church of the Palatinate" (Germany) or "The Mission-Covenant Church of Sweden" does not affect my present argument because their close relations with the traditional Congregationalists and with the International Congregational Council have dated only from the past ten years or so.

I believe that it is easier for us to enter into fruitful ecumenical discourse if we retain our traditional interpretation of the word "Church" than if we follow other bodies in calling ourselves collectively "a church," using the word as it is used in "The Church of England," "The Presbyterian Church," or "The Church of Scotland." This is because we can present to those with whom we are conversing a church order, symbolized in a church terminology, which expresses very well both our assurance that our churchmanship has a sound New Testament basis, and our admission that as a body we lack that catholicity which is the mark of the church universal.

We cannot call ourselves a catholic church: but we are much affronted by those who, being members of a communion which does not include all Christians (and which they admit, as of sound catholic doctrine, does not include all Christians) call themselves catholic. We believe not only that *we* are in schism but that the Church as a whole is in schism. Our preference for a cautious word like "Union" (or "Synod") rather than a conclusive one like "Church" expressed, when that was our habit of speech, our acknowledgement of our part in this imperfect state of things.

If the Congregationalists of England and English-speaking Wales elect to call themselves not a "union" but a "church," the term will be justifiable in that it expresses (or is intended to express) a closer relation between individual churches than is expressed by "union"; and in as much as this is a gesture against irrational and anarchic independency, it is wholly to be welcomed. In 1954 the Congregational Union of England and Wales declared in effect that independency which equalled perverse unneighbourliness was a sin, and stressed by this the fact that "independent" historically means only independent of the State, and of any kind of Establishment.[1]

But the mischief that the word "church" might do outweighs (in my view) its advantages as a symbol private to Congregationalists. For it might well give to other communions the impression that Congregationalism is entrenching itself in a more settled denominational position. It might even appear to be a status-symbol. And it might give the impression that we believe ourselves to be a catholic church. I do not myself hold that we can ever do this. If I imply by this that the use of the word "church" by other communions in this sense is a wrong use, I am stating a traditional Congregationalist view, and am prepared to stand by it, displeasing though it might appear to members of those other communions.

The corollary of the view I am here expounding is that

[1] After all, when Cromwell called himself an Independent, he meant that he was independent not only of the Anglican establishment which he was fighting, but also of the Presbyterian establishment implied in the findings of the Westminster Assembly.

Congregationalism is not a church but an order within the church catholic. I am assuming that Congregationalists have something to say, that only they can speak of from historic experience, to the other communions: and that this that they are saying must remain a lively element in the thinking of any united church (government by friendship). But I am also assuming that in most parts of the rest of the church there are people who will hear this and understand it easily. There may even be many who say that it is nothing new (though such persons must be warned against believing too hastily that they understand it). And if it comes eventually to be thought that there is a place in the catholic church for an order of persons who are especially skilled in this form of church action—a form which in times of national emergency (as was found in Germany a generation ago) proves to be the only workable form of church order—then this is the place which in such a catholic church Congregationalists could at once take.

I shall therefore refrain here from ever describing the body of Congregationalists collectively as "a church."[1]

[1] When the matter was under discussion in March 1961, the eminent New Testament scholar, Dr. G. B. Caird, was invited to comment on the proposed use of the word "church" in Congregationalism. His published comment is based on the appearance in the New Testament of the word "church" as meaning not only the local gathering of Christians, but a larger gathering which was yet not the whole company of Christians. The specific example is at Laodicea, where we hear of "a church" of Laodicea, and also "a church" in the house of Nympha, who lived in Laodicea. Dr. Caird thus argues that on an N. T. basis we need not be tied to the double definition I have cited here as traditional. He further says, "Can we honestly say that all activities proper to the church's life are discharged within the local congregation? If not, we need not hesitate to use the word "church" to describe the larger fellowship of which the local congregation (the church in Nympha's house) is a part.

But I am disposed to ask whether this sufficiently takes account of the sorrows of schism. There is no schism between the church at Nympha's, the church in Laodicea, and the whole company of Christians. I base my doubt about this on the improbability that an N.T. writer would ever have spoken, in the context of 1 Corinthians 1, of "the church" of Paul, "the church" of Apollos, and "the church" of Cephas.

### The danger of arguing from Scripture

Many Congregationalists would wish to say, I believe, that there is much more than this that a united church would stand to gain if Congregationalists were comprehended in it. Some, for example, would want to say that Congregationalism is their order because they believe it to be more faithful to the pattern of the New Testament than any other. While it is true that historically this is one of the strongest reasons why Congregationalism formed itself, at this time of day it would be idle and presumptuous for us to disregard the views of those who hold that the faithful interpretation of the New Testament must not disregard the movement of history, and must not be so literal-minded as to lose the spirit for the sake of the letter. It is not now so difficult as it once was for Congregationalists to understand those who claim equal faithfulness for other forms of church order. On the whole I should not wish to argue this case on Biblical grounds, because there is sufficient example in the past history of Christianity in England to show us how sterile and acrimonious argument from the text of Scripture to the church's practice can become.

### Culture

Again, it was inevitable that the history of Congregationalism should produce an *ethos* which some might think distinguishes Congregationalists from other British Christians. Some might wish to mention independence and flexibility of mind, an aptitude for New Testament scholarship, a sense of political responsibility, a moral rectitude, a disinclination for what is formal and artificial—qualities some of which contradict others, but all of which could easily be applied, or have been applied, to Congregationalists of this or of past generations. But while such an argument might have carried some weight fifty years ago, so much has happened during the twentieth century to bring the Congregationalist culture closer to that of other Christians that the ground is now too unstable to erect any argument on. Those who wish to read a lively exposition of the culture of Congregationalism to-day must read *Congregationalism, a Restatement*, by Daniel Jenkins (Faber, 1954): indeed, a study of that book is indispensable for all those of other ways who would understand ours.

But in one matter there is something to be said which will certainly be said in other ways by the apologists of other non-Anglican denominations: this is in the field of worship.

### Customs in Worship

Here perhaps we encounter the most powerful force in the present controversy between the communions. Where there is now much conversation at other levels in perfect harmony, and much eager learning from one another, our ritual customs continue to provide a dangerous hazard in the road of ecumenical progress. Two matters, of course, must at once be distinguished.

On the one hand, there is the sacramental controversy, which is closely linked with the differing doctrines of the ministry. That I shall set aside for the moment, and return to in my next chapter. On the other hand there is the profoundly different "feel" of worship that an Anglican experiences when he attends a Congregational (or otherwise non-established) church. In order not to overlap what others will be writing, I must try to confine myself here to what is especially Congregational in the habits of worship to which we are accustomed. It is obvious that there is a wider difference between the whole worship-ethos of the free churches and Anglican worship than there is between different free-church communions. It is in this field that the Methodist Connexion is clearly the "bridge-church," comprising as it does traditions which are very near that of the prayer-book, and traditions also of the freest sort. Within other denominations—certainly within Congregationalism—there is a similar, though not so wide, variety of practice. But unless one looks carefully at the matter in an ecumenical context one is liable to miss certain fine but important distinctions of level at which differences occur. This is no place to discuss comparative liturgies; it is these differences of level that are here important.

Certain Congregational habits are, of course, the direct outcome of historic controversy. Very little is actually known of the worship-habits of primitive Congregationalists in the time of Browne and Barrow. But what is evident to everybody is that once it had been finally decided in 1662 that conformity to the Book of Common Prayer as revised in that year was to be the test of eligibility for any legal ministry, Dissenters would steer very clear of the Prayer Book and all it stood for.

Worship in Congregationalism has in fact passed through several stages. The first—during the time of the ejectment (1662–89) and for a while after—is that in which worship was entirely free and informal, centred on the exposition of the Bible and adorned with extempore prayer. In those days any use of a book of any sort was regarded as treachery to those who "gave up their livings rather than obey the demand to use the Book of Common Prayer" (I deliberately over-simplify the history, of which in other places I have written). During the eighteenth century a cerebral emphasis in Congregationalist worship made itself felt, more weight being given to the sermon, and less to the "family-prayers" tradition. Later still, as a consequence of the evangelical revival, large churches brought a romantic element into public worship, a development of the preacher as artist rather than as lecturer, a subtle transforming of the congregation into an actor's rather than a lecturer's audience, with an attendant rising interest in church music, especially hymnody. This in turn brought a new consciousness of liturgic aesthetic, which gained ground slowly in the nineteenth century, but with rapidly increased impetus in the twentieth. In our own time we are in an age of sacramental revival (which we share with all other free-churchmen) and of the reassessment of liturgy on dogmatic rather than aesthetic grounds. So that at present we have several directories of public worship, a fading of the tradition of extempore prayer, a depression of the sermon from its former height of artistry to something more didactic than symbolic, a marked interest in the higher forms of church music, and a movement towards more frequent Communion and more dogmatically-based Baptism. (In England it is the normal custom to celebrate the Communion twice monthly: but more than one church now celebrates every Sunday.)

All this is very natural: but in ecumenical encounter it is confusing, because different Congregationalists stand at different points in the line of development, and perhaps no single Congregationalist regards all the developments here briefly sketched as desirable steps. In what I am about to say it will be evident that at least one of them seems to be undesirable.

If the content of our contribution in worship is to be

simplified to its furthest point, it must be stated under three heads: what we believe about prayer, about preaching, and about the Lord's Supper—taking this last at the level of ritual for the moment, and still leaving aside sacramental doctrine.

## Public Prayer

Concerning prayer, however much we may have experimented in approximating our services to Matins and Evensong in some places, our true doctrine still remains very far from that which in the Church of England is traditional. Our tradition of free prayer—which is now held to embrace "extempore prayer," prepared and unscripted prayer, prepared and specially-written prayer, or prayer specifically chosen from some written source—is very different from the tradition of "Common Prayer." Whatever else we do, normally our prayers are different, entirely different, one Sunday from what they were the previous Sunday. All our prayers, you might say, are "propers," though they are not always seasonal. Whatever method is used, we appear to deny the principle of common prayer, which resides precisely in that familiarity which, we tend to assume, breeds contempt. The characteristic emphasis of Congregational (and other puritan) worship leads us to reject the idea of the *opus dei*, the Church's continual routine of prayer and praise, in favour of the idea of every Sunday being a great and unique occasion—the celebration of the Lord's Resurrection. While it would be foolish to imagine that every Sunday is not a great day to men of the catholic mind, Congregational habit has led us traditionally to make less distinction between Sundays, but to distinguish them more decidedly from weekdays, than does the catholic tradition.

There is virtually no weekday worship in the puritan tradition—which historically reserves weekday worship for the home. Weeknight meetings for devotion are not infrequent: but they are regarded as special and rather intimate occasions, not as a continuation of the work that was begun on Sunday. At this point it might well be said that the puritan ethos has lost touch with a society in which the family is so much less significant a unit than it was in the seventeenth century, and in which the community has so largely supplanted the family. That charge, I think, lies against us. It lies especially because we have lost whatever technique we had of family worship. This is a point at which we most evidently need the help of our brothers in other traditions.

### Preaching

But it has produced one thing which we believe to be precious; this is the preaching tradition. Since puritan ethos leaned so heavily on the Bible, and so little on church teaching, puritan preaching has always been strictly bible-based. Traditionally much has been expected of the puritan preacher, and he has felt free to give much. This tradition persists also, of course, in the Church of Scotland as well as in other English Free Church communions. The major difference between the Anglican sermon and the puritan one is simply that the Anglican sermon may well be based on part of the teaching of the Prayer Book (the Catechism, or a Collect, for example), while a puritan sermon could never be. True—some thirty years ago it was common for Congregationalist sermons to be based neither on Prayer Book nor on Bible, but on some literary or scientific tag.

But my central point is that traditionally Congregationalists have regarded the sermon as a great, almost as a sacramental, occasion, and it is only recently that the great art of preaching has suffered depreciation in our midst.

I should not dream of asserting that there are no fine preachers in the Church of England. But it is undeniable that on the whole in the Parish Church or Cathedral the congregation (partly no doubt because it has so much richer a context for its devotional response to the Gospel) not only demands less of its preachers, but would be positively uncomfortable if it were met Sunday by Sunday with the continuous high pressure of preaching which until recently was expected in Congregationalism.

Put plainly, the fact is that a random Anglican who entered a Congregational church would be as incapable of feeling that a fine sermon (as Congregationalists thought it) compensated for the barrenness of the liturgy (as he would think it), as a Congregationalist would be of thinking that the splendour of Cranmer's prose and the glory of medieval architecture compensated for a trivial discourse from the pulpit. This is a point at which ecumenical encounter will, among the rank and file, be costly indeed.

### The Sacraments

Concerning the Sacraments of Baptism and the Lord's Supper, there are, especially in the second, large differences of custom which would appear odd to those who use other customs. Of baptism, however, it is primarily necessary to note that those suggested reforms of the rite which are at present being offered in the Anglican communion[1] are to

[1] See *Baptism and Confirmation* A Report submitted by the Church of England Liturgical Commission to the Archbishops of Canterbury and York (S.P.C.K., 1959).

Free Churchmen, and perhaps especially to Congregationalists, a matter for the greatest satisfaction. It is, and has long been, the Congregationalist custom to baptize infants not at a private service but in the course of (or less recently at the end of) Morning Service. Private baptism, characteristically, where it has been practised (in the North of England and until quite recently in Scottish Congregationalism) has been administered not in the church but in the home. However, our traditional doctrine, now largely recovered, is that baptism shall be administered in the presence of the whole congregation; and the movement away from the familiar afternoon christenings of the parish churches is one with which we should, of course, be wholly in sympathy.

As to the Communion, however, there is much more that needs to be explained. Our custom is to administer the Sacrament to the congregation seated in the pews, and almost universally it is administered in the form of small cubes of ordinary bread and small glasses of non-alcoholic wine. The minister distributes the elements from behind the Communion-table, and they are borne to the congregation by members of the diaconate (who may be men or women). The liturgy that accompanies this act is now much fuller than it was a generation ago, but is still by prayer-book standards somewhat brief and is, of course, not bound to prescribed words. The Words of Institution (from I *Cor.* II) are used, I imagine, almost invariably now; but what other words are used are either suggested in directories of worship or selected by the minister for himself.

It is not too much to say that almost all of this will be repellent to those who are brought up on the Anglican Eucharist. The inconspicuousness of the table, the omission of so many familiar words, the loss of the procession to the communion-rail, the absence of the common cup, the substitution of non-alcoholic wine for true wine, the apparent casualness of sitting rather than kneeling at the reception of the elements—all this added together would make an Anglican feel that virtually nothing of what he understood by communion was left.

But here is where we should ask such a person to pause while we do our best to explain. The root of all these customs (and, of course, it is the duty of Congregationalists to see that this is made very evident, and not obscured, by their ritual habits) is in the Congregationalist view of the Church. While no weight is taken from the emphasis which the Church universally places on the Lord's Supper as an act of communion with the Lord, Congregationalism insists on a parallel emphasis on it as an act of communion by men with one another.

It is fatally easy to miss this, or to obscure it. The way in which it is made evident in Congregationalism is by ensuring that the members of the congregation serve one another, and are not served separately by the deacons, with the elements. Here I mention a fact which is largely overlooked in present-day Congregationalism, and although I wish to suppress internal controversies in this essay, I am bound to say that I think it important for ecumenical reasons that this act of reception by and from members be insisted on. This in turn derives from the doctrine of the "priesthood of all believers," another doctrine which we commonly make less intelligible than it should be; for (as we shall see) it is not Congregationalist doctrine that anybody can be a minister of the Gospel: but it is our doctrine that not episcopal ordination but the fact of having covenanted with the Lord and with His neighbour gives a man the right to serve his neighbour with these holy things; our communion custom therefore attempts to preserve the intimacy and augustness of the Last Supper without over-emphasizing the privateness of the act.

I think that during the past thirty years we have reached a position in which an Anglican visitor might wish to reciprocate the satisfaction which I just now attributed to Congregationalists who observe the Anglican baptismal reforms. Without doubt our customs did corrupt themselves grievously: but the movement to-day is towards the restoration of the Supper to its primary place as the central act of worship, towards the stressing of the Resurrection as its first cause, rather than the memorial and even funereal note which used commonly to be sounded, and towards the enrichment of the liturgy by the recall of classic Calvinist liturgical precedents. This is in its way an "Oxford movement" in Congregationalism, which has brought us much nearer than we were to the sacramental practice of those of Catholic and Anglican mind: although it is evident to none more than ourselves that there is still a very great gulf between us. It is, however, the symbolism of the *koinonia*, the communion in the spirit, which we believe to be indispensable to the Supper, and which we should bring to a united church (as we have brought to the Church of South India).

Now somebody will doubtless say, "But the Communion is a sacrament of unity: and you have perverted it." And we must not fall into the trap of dismissing this objection by saying, "But we observe and exemplify more decisively than you do the communion of men with one another," because the proper reply from the other side will then be "Yes: but only within your four walls." Congregationalists must never lose their vigilance at this point. Customs which are in themselves gracious and are hallowed by long usage may none the less express a partial or even corrupt theology; and in particular, those customs which arise from the felicities of the "gathered church" must not be allowed to provide ground for indifference to the missionary and evangelical commitment of the Church.

### Social factors in the development of Worship

There are, however, certain other aspects of Congregationalist worship and church custom which arise rather from social than from theological causes. These will be equally apparent to a visitor from a different communion, although again they are normally to be found in other Free Church communions. I refer here to such things as our rather free use of hymns, and correspondingly restricted use of sung psalms and choral pieces. Much has resulted from our lack of anything in church music corresponding to a "cathedral tradition"—that is, a continuing pattern of ritual excellence which sets a standard for local practice. An Anglican visitor to our worship would find it somewhat overweighted with one form of congregational song—the hymn. What psalms and anthems were sung, he would probably find somewhat vulgar in musical appointment, and except in very wealthy and populous churches, indifferently rendered. The puritan tradition restricted church music on principle. The romantic tradition of the nineteenth century extended it for aesthetic satisfaction. It provides now in most Free Churches, and not least in Congregationalism, a strange mixture of uninhibited naturalism and Calvinistic narrowness. This is not the place to go further into this special matter: but the origin of difference at this point is as much social as theological.

So is the origin of the now admitted ugliness and inadequacy of many of our buildings. Puritan opinion prescribed an unpretentious building, following standards of architecture that were domestic rather than public. Romantic expansion produced very large and commanding buildings, most of which were put up in the age of commercial building, and exhibit more pomp than love. The arrangement of their furniture—the central pulpit and closely-packed pews—combines theological origin with social fashion: a central pulpit exalts the preacher as a consequence of exalting preaching; the packed pews indicate the hope of a very large congregation economically accommodated. Trivial and important values mix themselves up in our emerging customs, and it is necessary for us to improve that judgement which will discern between what is and what is not of value in ecumenical encounter. (See further pp. 72–76.)

Our manners in church—our tendency to be less silent before and after service and much more silent during its progress—are similarly the result of a mixture of motives. On the other hand, our people chatter to one another because they are liable to know one another particularly well, and their building offers no accommodation for social intercourse at that moment apart from the sanctuary itself: on the other, our tradition ascribes less objective "holiness" to buildings and their furniture, placing more religious emphasis on the friendship that causes people to chatter in that irritating way than on the sense of religious awe which would forbid it "in church." Half of this is important: the other half is easily dispensed with. We value the friendship: there is no reason to value the unimaginatively conceived accommodation or the self-conscious cheapness and ugliness of so much of our furniture.

# 5

# Hard Points of Controversy

IT is now necessary to look briefly at certain matters of controversy between Congregationalists and other denominations which have proved up to now the most intractable. These are points of doctrine rather than consequences of custom. Taking the broadest possible view, Congregationalists are probably at odds with Roman Catholics and with some Anglicans on the doctrine of the Lord's Supper and on the doctrine of the Ministry. It is here, anyhow, that we always come to a stand when we engage in conversation.

I am obliged always to use such a word as "probably," because of one characteristic of Congregationalism which others, especially Anglicans and Roman Catholics, find (understandably) very irritating. This is that it is never very easy to extract a proposition in purely doctrinal form from a Congregationalist body. On the one hand, there is no doctrine of the Creed of Nicaea which Congregationalists, *qua* Congregationalists, are obliged to disbelieve. But on the other, it is always as difficult to answer the question "What is the Congregational *doctrine* about this?" as it is easy to answer the question, "What is the Congregational *custom* about that?" It would perhaps be going too far to say that all Congregational doctrine is case-law; but it certainly is true that when, for example, it was thought wise to try to decide what Congregationalists as a whole had to say about divorce, it was necessary to abandon the hope of producing a unanimous document, or, indeed, anything more than a highly inconclusive and unhelpful report.

The fact is that on the question of divorce, the very large majority of Congregational ministers agree that the re-marriage of divorced persons is not inadmissible in church; but you may always come across one who holds a rigorist view, and who is not considered less a Congregationalist for doing so. But that is merely an example.

### Doctrine of the Ministry

What do we believe about the Ministry? Here it is possible to state a basic belief, dissent from which would involve a Congregationalist in contradiction. It is contained in the following words from the Confession of Faith appended to the *Savoy Declaration* of 1658:

> XI. The way appointed by Christ for the calling of any person, fitted and gifted by the Holy Ghost, unto the office of Pastor, Teacher or Elder in a Church, is, that he be chosen thereunto by the common suffrage of the Church it self, and solemnly set apart by Fasting and Prayer, with the Imposition of Hands of the Eldership of that Church, if there be any before constituted therein. . . .
>
> XII. The Essence of this Call of a Pastor, Teacher or Elder unto Office, consists in the Election of the Church, together with his acceptation of it, and separation by Fasting and Prayer: and those who are so chosen, though not set apart by Imposition of Hands, are rightly constituted Ministers of Jesus Christ, in whose name and Authority they exercise the Ministery to them so committed. . . .

It has already been shown (above, pp. 16–21) how the

foreground of this has suffered modification due to changing circumstances. But the essence of this doctrine is still firmly held, and it resists any form of episcopal ordination. It similarly resists any claim to special grace through the Apostolic Succession. The resistance to episcopacy itself, be it noted, comes from nothing specifically stated in the *Savoy Declaration*: but that is because the declaration, being based on the Westminster Confession, assumes a church order that is non-episcopal, and independent of Apostolic Succession.

### Ordination

Nowadays, of course, Congregationalists do not wish to say, as their founding fathers said with truculent persistence, that episcopal orders are no orders at all. But they resist firmly any implication on the part of those who follow an episcopal system that their orders are no orders. This position they hold as derived directly from the practice of the most primitive Church: ministers are ministers in as much as, having manifested the gifts of the Spirit, they are set aside to their task by the Church. The Church they take to be not those who have (or claim) a spiritual descent directly from the apostles, but the gathered and covenanted fellowship of believers in a given place.

Let it be admitted that it was the apostles who performed the first ordinations, that Philip was sent to Samaria from Jerusalem, not ordained at Samaria. Such an admission is damaging to the Congregationalist case in so far as that case is built entirely on a biblical foundation. But this is not the first time that it has had to be agreed, in this brief essay, that arguments built on the text of Scripture are doomed to be divisive. The real reason for the Congregationalists' rejection of episcopal ordination is their recollection of the corruptions which historically vitiated the episcopate in their fathers' minds.

In fact, as doctrine has developed since 1658, it has become the custom of Congregationalists to conduct their ordinations always in the local churches, but always also in the presence of some significant representative of the wider fellowship of churches. It is in this capacity that the Moderator takes part, if he does take part; and if he does not, it is unusual, and is generally thought a defect, if the ordination takes no account at all of the wider fellowship, and if no such representative (for example, of the County Union) is invited to take part in it.

Congregationalists at present resist episcopal doctrine for one primary reason: that as things stand at present, if any minister of theirs sought to minister in an episcopal church, it would be required that he be reordained. We have no right to be indignant if we are required to be "re-commissioned" (as was done in the Church of South India); but for it to be implied that in the eyes of some we have been masquerading as ministers when we were not ministers seems to us unjust and unhistorical. Any union with episcopals would bring great cost which we ought to be quite ready to bear; much of it is a cost for which we are morally responsible as schismatics. But we are not yet persuaded that in rejecting the Apostolic succession we have been practising a deceit on our congregations. Nor, of course, do our neighbours really believe it. This is a doctrinal point in which penitence alone will bring honourable settlement.

The relation between Congregational orders and those of other communions can be expressed only in a double statement: a statement, that is, one half of which expresses what Congregationalists intend, and the other half, what others accept. It is well known that our orders are accepted by Methodists and Baptists as not debarring us from occasional ministry in their churches, and that in England they are accepted by Presbyterians (since 1956) as being in all respects on equal standing with their own, so that ministers in the two communions can be regarded as inter-available. On the other hand they are formally rejected by Anglicans and by Roman Catholics.

From our side, this is what is to be said. At a full ordination, the minister is ordained to the ministry and Sacraments, and inducted to the pastorate of this church in which he is being ordained. That is: his authority to minister *here* is authenticated by the call of the local church, symbolically stated in the course of the service through one of its office-bearers. His authority to minister in *any* church of ours is authenticated by the presence and participation in our service of one or more ecumenical office-bearers (usually, as I have said, the Moderator, but other officers may be present in his stead or by his side). So far as we are concerned, we commend by this act our ordained minister to any church which may call him to minister—not only to this one, but to any of our union: and not only to those, but to any of any other communion which may deem him worthy of call. On this ground we make in ordination a public statement that entitles the minister to be called "Reverend" in public address, and requires no fresh ordination when he removes to another charge. We feel that if he moved into a united church, fresh ordination should not be required; but we are obliged at present to accept the consequences of other views on this matter.

The double statement of ordination leaves room for the working of a more limited ministry. It is always possible for a minister to be called by a local church without being, in our contemporary sense, made by that call a publicly ordained minister. We require of the ordained minister certain evidences of his fitness to perform his office, some of which are spiritual but others of which are academic; he must have satisfied the elders of the Congregational Union of an adequate training either by producing a certificate that he has completed a college course, or by passing certain examinations set by the committee of the union charged with that duty. This on the one hand: on the other, of course, he must produce some kind of statement as to his spiritual fitness and the authenticity of his calling to be a minister.

On the second of these, of course, there is little check; and it goes without saying that if there is any doubt about spiritual fitness, a candidate would not be accepted for training, and would not be deemed suitable to minister in any circumstances. But it is always possible that a man of limited training but much personal grace may commend himself to a local community, and be capable of excellent pastoral and teaching work among those who are his friends, although he does not have, or claim to have, the equipment for a more public or generalized form of ministry. Moreover, country congregations in our order would often be left without any kind of ministry were they debarred from calling to their pulpits men of devout mind who make their living in other ways, but perform an adequate part-time ministry among the small local flock. It is understandable that the churches as a whole might not wish to commend such men, of limited training and outlook, to be ministers at large; but the Congregational principle that a church may call any man to be its minister who manifests in its eyes the gifts of the Spirit is here respected. "Evangelists," as these are called, were until recently distinguished by being enrolled on a separate list of ministers in the official Year Book of the Union. That custom has now changed (I refrain from comment on the change), but the principle remains.

The Congregational principle can, of course, be abused. It is possible for a local congregation to call to its ministry a man who in the eyes of the Elders of the Union is morally or doctrinally an unsuitable person. If it deems it necessary, the Union can withdraw its recognition both from the pastor and from the church concerned. This, of course, rarely happens.

On the whole our system is logical, though its application is sometimes less so. Details are here irrelevant; but members of other communions can be told that Congregationalists at present recognize the necessity of stating at ordination not only the authenticity of a man's call to a local ministry, but their commendation of him as a minister to all who will hear him.

### Development of the classic doctrine

Two other subsidiary points need to be mentioned in regard to the ministry. In the first place, as a consequence of our present doctrine of ordination, our practice has developed to an extent dangerous to the literal preservation of the ideals of Savoy. It was held implicitly until quite recently that only a gathered church could ordain, and therefore it was only to a pastorate that a minister could be ordained. In fact, all those senior members of our ministry who at present hold offices of ecumenical nature—professors, secretaries of missionary or inter-church organizations, even publishers and teachers—began their lives as pastors. But it is now recognized that a minister can be Congregationally ordained to an ecumenical office directly. Ordinations have recently been conducted from which men proceeded direct to a post with the S.C.M., or a students' chaplaincy. What then in Congregationalist view constitutes the ordaining principle here? It is quite simple. The local church, wherever it is, ordains, and at once *sends*. But the ordination is still in a local church; all that is added is a missionary touch such as was unprovided for in the seventeenth-century scheme of things.

## Ordination of Women

The other point, which brings dispute in ecumenical discussion, is of course that of the ordination of women. It is wise for Congregationalists to recognize that the position is not properly stated by saying that only they and the Baptists give women ecclesiastical status. But it is true that only they permit the Sacrament of the Lord's Supper to be ordinarily dispensed by a woman.

The ordination of women to a ministry similar in all respects to that for which men may be ordained is, in Congregationalism, a derived rather than an ancient practice. As I have elsewhere remarked, such ordination is not provided for in the seventeenth-century documents, and it may be suspected that the only reason why it is not provided against is that its possibility never occurred to the authors of those documents. The puritan tradition is very far from feminist. In fact, the first woman minister in Congregationalism was ordained in 1917. In the discussions which are being at present held between Congregationalists in Scotland and the Church of Scotland, the eligibility of women for the ministry is proving to be a point on which Congregationalists are unwilling to yield. And it may be observed that the unwillingness of the Presbyterians in Scotland and the Anglicans in England to ordain women has resulted in the movement of certain women from those churches into Congregationalism in order that they might fulfil what they believed to be their proper calling. At least one woman in England is at present ministering with success, and more than one in Scotland, having come from a background of the national church.

Most Congregationalists are in no doubt of the propriety of their view on this. A few are in doubt, and I confess to being myself among them. But although the ordained woman is a relatively modern phenomenon in our churches, it is evident that it must follow from our doctrine that the call of a local church is the authenticating principle of ministry that any person so "called" is eligible without reference to sex.

The basis of the rejection of women's ordination in the Church of England appears to be somewhat different from that in the Church of Scotland. But both have an order of deaconesses, although the quasi-Catholic revival in the Church of England has made it possible for that communion to go much further, for example, in the establishment of contemplative and teaching convents, than Scotland has been able to go.

One thing is quite clear, however, and that is that the Congregational way, in opening the ministry to women, has not proved to be conducive to a very resourceful or appropriate use of the denomination's woman-power. Not a large proportion of ordained women serve long in the pastorate. Between the pastorate and the service of women on local diaconates (a status which would be itself denied to women in the Church of Scotland, where they may not be Elders) there is no way in which we can offer to a woman such opportunity as can be found in the Methodist, Anglican or Roman communions of giving full-time consecrated service to the church—with one exception, which has significantly appeared since 1945. This is the woman "missioner" trained at St. Paul's House, Liverpool, who is not ordained as a minister, but who is specially sent to some emergency-spot (a church on a new estate, or a near-derelict downtown church) to do intensive work on a short-term basis which may prepare the way for a full ministry in that place. This is excellent: but in any discussion of this vexatious problem we must be ready to learn from more ancient traditions, even where they appear to us somewhat levitical in their prohibitions.

"The Laity"

What, however, may be regarded as a legitimate consequence, and a desirable one, of Congregationalism's teaching about the ministry and the eldership (which traditionally, as Savoy shows, are very close) is a certain traditional sense of lay responsibility in religious matters which is evident in all forms of Dissent, and perhaps slightly less evident in the established churches. It is a matter of common knowledge that in such a movement as "Kirk Week" in Scotland, which deliberately sets out to be a movement for the recovery of responsibility in the laity, Congregationalism, a small denomination, has provided a lay impetus out of all proportion to its small size. It is traditional in England for the government of Congregationalism to be less clerically dominated than that of the Church of England: but here again the distinction is far less sharp than it was fifty years ago, since the shortage of leisured laymen in Congregationalism has come at the same time as an upsurge of lay feeling in the Church of England. We are, in fact, more, and they less, clerical than was formerly the case.

Of laymen's ministry in the specific sense of lay-pastorates and lay-preaching Congregationalism in England has much experience (in Scotland it has hardly any). But the real source of lay-preaching is, of course, Methodism, and Congregationalism's lay ministry is an imitation of that upon which Methodism leans so heavily. It is best, therefore, for me to leave that subject to the Methodist writer in this series.

One last point concerning our ministry and its practical problems might be inserted here, although it is not a dogmatic one. It is one of the signs of Congregationalism's defective catholicity that it has taken so long for its members to recognize that patterns of ministry may vary. I have just referred to the new practice of ordaining otherwise than to a pastoral charge. What Congregationalism has lost through its inability (partly economic, partly temperamental) to sustain canonries may well be something quite substantial. All ministers, to most minds in the rank and file of Congregationalism, are men who visit the sick, preach twice a Sunday, administer the sacraments, and direct the Church Meeting in local churches. The idea of setting any aside for special work which comprises some but not all of these activities—or perhaps none—is not only impracticable in a denomination whose economics are so restricted: it is somewhat against its settled temper of mind, which tends to be puritan and activist and impatient of square pegs. Our only collegiate communities are those which are explicitly centred on our theological colleges: and these communities are always woefully small and hard-worked. The consequence is that our theology is very nearly all written by the staffs of our colleges; and that men whose gifts are unusual, but deficient at certain practical points (for example, the easy mixing that makes a successful pastor), either do not offer themselves for our ministry, or have a very uncomfortable time in it, and later leave it. The more remote abuses that are consequent on this I will not here enumerate, although my sojourn in academic life introduced me to many of them. This inelasticity breeds powerful pastors and preachers: but it leaves little room for contemplative Dissent.

By the same token—and here all non-Roman Catholic Christians are over against those of Rome—there can be little doubt that our acceptance of a married ministry has had the effect of leaving us with very few trained or perceptive lay theologians. There are exceptions, but on the whole Dissenting theology is written by tutors, and Anglican theology by priests: whereas Roman Catholic theology is not infrequently written at the highest level by laymen. The idea that a man can be a theologian without being a priest is naturally likely to have greater currency in a communion where the priesthood is celibate. It is a tolerable (although to Dissent not an acceptable) notion that the priesthood should be celibate; but nobody need say that marriage is incompatible with theological study. It just happens that where the ministry is not thus very specially selected, theological thinking is left to ministers. This cannot be a gain.

### Doctrine of the Lord's Supper

Concerning the Lord's Supper and its doctrines, once

again it is fair to say that the ordinary Congregationalist is more concerned about his own exclusion from the table of his Anglican brothers than about the retention of any positive doctrine of the Sacrament. At one time it would have been possible to speak more plainly than one can now speak of distinctive Congregational doctrine. It is still true, of course, that the doctrine that Congregationalists hold and express is derived from, or at least not contradictory of, Reformed doctrine. They do not hold that at the offering of the Elements the sacrifice of Calvary is repeated—in which doctrine they follow Calvin and not the Council of Trent; and they resist any doctrine of transubstantiation, and are suspicious of such practices as "reservation" which appear to imply that kind of doctrine. These two matters, the denial of the repeated sacrifice and the denial of transubstantiation, are still points at which they would be in controversy with some Anglicans and all Roman Catholics; in no point of doctrine are they at variance with their fellow nonconformists (although as has been said, at certain points of practice they differ from them).

There is a point, of course, at which the doctrines of the ministry and of the Sacrament of the Lord's Supper converge. Congregationalists, believing in the authentication of "call" by the local church, have no doctrine which obliges a church to have its Sacrament administered by a man in orders. Traditionally, there is nothing to prevent its being administered, and regularly administered, by laymen or women. This is because we do not hold that this kind of special grace (which enables a man validly to administer) is conferred at ordination, but rather that the call of the local church at that time to administer is sufficient vehicle of the necessary grace.

None the less, there is a strong feeling throughout Congregationalism that it is more *seemly* that a minister perform this sacred task, and that it should be done by another only when no minister is available to do it. Thus in practice there is very little between the kind of emergency in which it seems proper in Congregationalism for a non-ordained person to administer and that in which it would be held tolerable in the Church of England; only in the matter of women is a door open in Congregationalism where it is firmly closed in Anglicanism.

But concerning the profounder doctrines of transubstantiation and of sacrifice, it seems best at the present stage of thinking to speak only with the greatest caution. Liturgical study and practice in Congregationalism are undergoing, as I write, a radical revival. What the end of this will be I do not care to judge. But nobody can read the work of the late Bernard Manning (for example) and still refer to Congregationalists (as Anglicans often used to do) as an "unsacramental" body. In the present state of affairs I am disposed to urge that all doors be left as wide open as they can be. Theological definitions are excellent and necessary sticks—but thoroughly unserviceable crutches. What, abiding by the letter of the Helvetic Confessions or the Westminster Confession, we claim to believe may well be not really what the Spirit urges us day by day to believe at all. We are liable, in our energetic defence of our principles, to attribute beliefs to others which they do not hold, or which they claim to hold only when we press them too far.

Specifically, although Reformed belief forbids us to think of the "repeated sacrifice," Congregationalists very generally hold a faith of the Eucharist that is much more than a mere memorialism. Their directories of worship, at least those published since 1940, evince a belief in the time-defying mystery of the Sacrament that reduces the controversy about repeated sacrifice to an argument about words. If, as we believe, the efficacy of Christ's Passion and Resurrection are here brought up into the present, while we would not say that *we* are offering a sacrifice which only He offered once for all, yet we are saying much more than that we are remembering or recollecting that sacrifice. The sense of worshipping "with the angels and archangels" is returning so strongly in our Eucharistic worship that our current hymn book prints (unhappily with an error) the words of the Canon which express this truth on the assumption that congregations will wish to use them: this, indeed, they widely do in England.

Again, while we have never countenanced that definition of the sacramental act which, by the Tridentine canon, says that at the consecration the substance is changed while the accidents remain unchanged, there are few Congregationalists who would regard the Elements, once used at Communion, as being thereafter suitable for profane use.[1] If

[1] Their disposal is a domestic problem which Congregationalists normally do not face. The bread used at Communion is ordinary bread, but having been "diced" for this special use, it is difficult to find any use for unconsumed quantities of it. It can be reasonably said that if the residue is put out for the birds to eat it is better used than if it be thrown to waste. The wine is non-alcoholic, and bottles in which it is delivered are commonly marked (with unconscious theological irony) "not to be used as a beverage." This problem is insoluble and it causes so much discomfort if it is raised that it is usually left unmentioned. It raises the whole question of the use of the common cup, and of alcoholic wine (obligatory in Catholic circles) at Communion: and this is not the place to discuss that. Meanwhile we find it best to regard the wine as symbolic, and as usable for no purpose but this sacred one, and to throw away what has been put out but not used. The best use to which bread could be put is, of course, that which could follow on the graceful and primitive practice that is sometimes to be seen in the Church of Scotland—that of passing a whole loaf, from which partakers take a share as they pass it: the remainder of the loaf could ideally be used at a common meal such as a "parish breakfast" thereafter. But "parish communion" has not yet come in Congregationalism. We are still in a state of tolerated anomaly in these matters.

there is anything "holy" or deserving of "reverence" in these things (and who can call any such conviction merely superstitious?) then we have some doctrine, even though it be unformulated, which we substitute for transubstantiation. Even this, then, is not necessarily a door finally closed. Charity should, if it suffers long enough and is kind enough, be productive of sufficient wisdom to carry us through either of these dogmatic difficulties. But the rising indignation, on both sides of the frontier, concerning the closing of Anglican tables to non-episcopally confirmed persons will break through the barrier, and perhaps do damage through lack of theological control, unless that matter is earnestly and wisely discussed, and soon.

# 6

# "Hard Facts of Unity"

ALL of us who are invited to write these books have been asked to take notice of Mr. John Lawrence's book, *The Hard Facts of Unity*. I observe that on page 112 of this book Mr. Lawrence writes (I abridge his paragraph):

> How many churches are ready to alter their mode of operation for the sake of unity? . . . Would the Free Churches agree to——well, I would rather the members of the Free Churches put their own questions to themselves.

Very well, then. Here are some of the questions a Congregationalist would need to set himself, which have not yet been mentioned.

## Councils of Churches

Gestures towards unity are best made, says Mr. Lawrence, in local communities. The levels at which these steps can be taken are, broadly speaking, in local councils of churches, in special co-operative ventures by ministers, and in the sharing of worship.

Local councils of churches have not been difficult to form, although too frequently their membership has stopped short of Roman Catholics and their deliberations have been less boldly controversial than they might have been. But I was myself, when a minister in the Black Country, a member of the Wednesbury Joint Council of Churches, which included not only Free Church ministers of all denominations alongside Anglicans of different complexions, but the staff of the Roman Catholic Church as well (the priest and his assistant). That had been in existence a year or two when I joined it in 1943. At certain of its meetings theological points of deep import were discussed freely; at others plans for united action were made. In the brief time that I was living there, one large public meeting was successfully held under the auspices of this Council.

Congregationalists at this level will have to ask themselves whether they will assent to the soft-pedalling of gestures of partial unity for the sake of gestures of total unity; for the decrease of the local Free Church Council (in England) or Fraternal (in Scotland) in order that the Joint Council may increase. This may turn out to be a hard question, because the banding together of people from churches superficially different but very largely sharing an ethos has turned out to be an easy—and on the whole an unprofitable—enterprise; unprofitable because so largely such bands at the Free Church level have encouraged Free Church unity at the expense of larger unity, and therefore positively encouraged the deepening of schism in the whole Church. Nothing much is lost, one supposes, by Congregationalists and Methodists mixing with one another, or Congregationalists and Presbyterians; but in England it is ten times as important that Congregationalists should meet and promote charity with Anglicans, and a hundred times as important (difficult in proportion) for them to promote charity with Roman Catholics. The organization of local Christian councils on the widest basis is the matter to which

Congregationalists ought to be prepared to devote much of the energy that goes into the organization at present of denominational efforts and interdenominational Free Church "get-togethers." At any rate, it is when the comprehensiveness of the ecumenical effort reaches that point that it begins to prove unpleasantly demanding. There, clearly, is the growing-point.

### Ministerial Encounter

It is equally evident that ministers should spend what time they can in one another's company at an ecumenical level. The extent to which this has increased in England and in Scotland is impressive. Fairly often now in new areas in England the evangelism of the neighbourhood is regarded as a joint enterprise by the local vicar and the local Free Church ministers. It can fairly be said that where the Congregationalists have been involved in this, they have not been the slowest to accept the demands of co-operation. Ever since the "council-estate" form of town planning came into existence, the Free Church Councils have at the local level continually expressed in their strategy a sense of the necessity of rationalizing their resources, and of not erecting new buildings in competition with one another in new regions. It is not always as easy as this. I can recall myself the reasonable desire of Congregationalists to erect and staff a new church in a new neighbourhood of one of England's "new towns," which was very strenuously, and even derisively, opposed by the Anglican incumbent. I can point to a new cause founded by Congregationalists in Scotland in a "new area" whose only claim to anybody's attention is that it is in competition with an extension church of the Church of Scotland; unstrategically placed, the cause has fallen on evil days within ten years of its foundation.

On the other hand, informal meetings between ministers of the Church of Scotland and Roman Catholic priests have been held, and publicly reported, during the past year or two, with spiritual consequences that all parties to the meetings agree in valuing most highly. It might well be that it is a pleasant obligation for a Congregational minister to observe the Week of Christian Unity by calling on the neighbouring Catholic priest. If it seemed good to him so to do, it is the duty of his congregation not to vilify him or spread foolish rumours; indeed, it might well be the duty of his congregation openly to state that such a visit should be paid at that season in their name, as a gesture of goodwill —for probably there are a few ministers who find themselves able to risk the consequences of such an action without the assurance that these will not be disastrous in their own churches.[1] The irrational hatred of Rome in which all Protestants shared a century ago is at present beginning to evaporate; anything that can be done to dissipate it, and to place controversy on rational lines, and to promote charity, must be regarded as a first-class priority. The way, I suspect, is somewhat harder in Scotland than it is in England; that is why the conversation between Scottish ministers and Roman Catholic priests is so significant a development just now.

Perhaps it is at the strictly local level that the greatest difficulties will arise, and here we have to face without shame and without fear the hazards of economics and vested interests.

## Economics

Economically, Congregationalism is (with the Baptists)

[1] I may perhaps say that I am so fortunately placed, and that this course of action is my habit during that January week.

the most independent and liberal of all the denominations. It is understood that the normal Congregational minister is maintained entirely by his people's voluntary gifts. It is further understood that only a very few Congregational churches have any kind of endowment. Apart from insignificant exceptions, the money comes into the plate at the church collection, and goes out through the church treasurer. To many this seems a very reasonable, Christian and "New Testament" way of ordering a church's economics. But none the less, it is patient of two uncomfortable comments.

First: it is now evident that some congregations are too poor and too small to carry the running expenses of a church including the minister's support and superannuation. Therefore since 1948 the Congregational Union of England and Wales has had a systematic "Home Churches Fund" into which all churches pay a contribution based on their size (in covenanted members), and out of which help is given to the weaker churches. The necessity was obvious when many ministers were living in poverty; and the adoption of this system of aid from the strong to the weak brought Congregationalism into line with contemporary practice in most other denominations.

But second: the emergence of those conditions which made the Home Churches Fund necessary exposed a certain characteristic of Independency about which some of its supporters might well be uneasy. This is the extent to which in former days small local churches were dependent for their economic existence on a few wealthy people. It was not a decline in membership that made the Home Churches Fund necessary. It was rather the disappearance from many of our smaller causes of senior folk who held virtually a controlling interest in them—an interest which their children did not inherit. On balance, and certainly from the ecumenical point of view, concentration of the church's resources in the hands of a few families, or even a single family, is a serious defect. Internally, it made dissent from the political or religious view of the controlling family virtually impossible for a minister who had no private means; in the recently published autobiography of the late D. R. Davies we see a good example of conditions which caused him to write of "the grave defect of the Free Church minister, that the minister is dependent for his bread and butter on the people to whom he preaches."[1] When one adds to this reflection the undeniable fact that the multiplication of schisms in the nineteenth century was closely connected with the multiplication of people who could financially afford to found them, one is left with very serious doubts whether the totally independent way of economics is a principle for which Congregationalism ought to expect Christians of other communions to make way.

However, it might be said on the other side that the freedom of a Congregational minister (provided he be not ministering in an "aided" church) to maintain himself and his family by adding to the earnings which his congregation can afford to pay him in such ways as writing or lecturing has produced in Congregationalism a number of exceptional, energetic and enterprising ministers who have made the best of the old-fashioned liberal notion of "incentive," and, by no means always to the detriment of their local pastorate and very often to the enrichment of the Church at large, have distinguished themselves in para-pastoral activities.

But all this is mentioned here only to elicit that comment on the economics of religious schism (which is in itself a

[1] *In Search of Myself* (1962), p. 63; cf. p. 90.

subject for a useful piece of research), and to lead on to the more pressing matter of vested interest in buildings and in local fellowships. And here, I think, three distinct points need to be made. There is the vested interest in the building or "plant"; the vested interest in the fellowship, and especially in its opportunity for the bearing of office; and there is a very strange, often unnoticed, but none the less powerful "class consciousness" in Dissent which amounts to a vested interest in inferiority.

### "A local habitation"

Congregational churches meet in buildings—some of which are antiquated, pretentious and unserviceable, but all of which command the affection of at any rate some of those who worship in them. Let union come in a district where there are within a quarter of a square mile half a dozen churches. Let two of these churches be actually facing one another on opposite sides of a street. Reason will insist that one of these (to go no further for the present) ought to close. The sight of two competing churches facing one another is a scandal. Which shall close? What happens to the office-bearers in the building that has closed? How can it be represented to them that it is for the good of the Kingdom that they, and not their opposite neighbour, should close? It is evident that if the congregation (be it only a small one) is to be uprooted, somebody will have to inspire in it a large sense of justice and an even more powerful sense of charity. Some people who were important in that fellowship will lose their status in the larger one. There will be no need, for example, in the combined church for two organists. Seniors who have given much of their time and loyalty and substance for the continuation of the separate cause must be persuaded that their time and substance have not gone to waste. Above all, the sense of loss that must come with the closing of the familiar building and the absence of some of the familiar voices must be compensated by a new kind of hope born of a lively doctrine (and a lively love) of the Church. The mischief is, of course, that the most likely victims of the "axe" will be small causes whose doctrine of the Great Church may well have been suffocated by the necessity for violent activism in keeping the place open, and by an absence of any liturgical tradition such as can always provide a rich source for this kind of hope and breadth of view.

### Ganging-up

The vested interest in the fellowship is that tendency of small groups to build up a very strong bond of friendship within their group, that correspondingly makes it difficult for the friends to make new friends. Congregational churches (as I have said) are proud of their prowess in local "love of the brethren." None of them should be invited to go back on their belief that this is one of the marks of the Church. But the family that is so united that none of its daughters may marry, and that the front door is never open to the visitor or the wayfarer, is not a good family or a Christian one. Friendship need not breed exclusiveness. We are strangers and pilgrims, and not everybody we meet in the way is necessarily an Amalekite bent on our destruction. Somehow the counterpoint of *agape* must be added to the harmony of internal friendship. For many this is going to be a difficult lesson. In a larger church unit the familiar personal landmarks disappear, and if gestures of unity are made the great danger is that the constituent bodies will for a long time remain as gangs or cliques producing block-votes in the larger body. It is going to help a great deal if those whose church-order has delivered them from these special dangers (and maybe from these special felicities) understand just what is bound to happen when Congregationalists respond to ecumenical overtures.

### Social Hazards

But now there is something much worse, and much more elusive, to be considered, and we must approach it obliquely in order to get the point made at all.

Fairly recently in a Scottish city the BBC approached a distinguished parish church (Church of Scotland) in order to make arrangements for broadcasting a service. It was thought wise and proper to invite the congregations of certain neighbouring churches to join in one of these services. This meant, of course, inviting the other churches to suspend their evening service and join in the united one. Of these neighbouring churches several were of the Church of Scotland, and certain others were of Dissent (I need not specify which denominations, but more than one were involved).

Arrangements were accordingly made. All those invited to participate did so. Their ministers were invited to take part in the service. The preacher was connected with none of the churches involved. A massive congregation met and joined in the worship.

Now it happened that in the inviting church there was an accomplished choir, which was asked to sing by itself at one point in the service. The choir wore robes. The choral piece chosen was a motet by an early seventeenth-century composer. In the invitation to join in the service, the BBC managed to convey ambiguous instructions about the choral arrangements, and in one of the invited churches (which was in Dissent) it was believed that members of its choir were invited to join the choir of the inviting church in singing this anthem. When certain of these choristers presented themselves at a final rehearsal, they were told that they could not be accommodated, and that in any case the anthem had been considerably rehearsed already, and additional voices at that stage would be unsuitable. All that was required of them was to its near the "home" choir and join in leading the hymns.

This caused grave offence. Another participating church was only delivered from this embarrassment by an intimation at the last moment that the choir would not be asked to go to the choir rehearsal, and the minister of *that* church took it on himself to explain that the reason was that choir-robes could not be found for more than the local choir. The intimation was made, and as I understand received, in a spirit of good-humoured resignation—"Oh, well, that's the sort of thing they do there: let 'em do it. We'll muck in." But it was only by accident that it occurred to that minister to make the necessary inquiry beforehand. The minister of the other church was left high and dry, and his people were embarrassed: and in fact they took considerable offence, believing that they had been in some way "elbowed aside," or slighted, by the inviting church.

This is a small and yet also a great matter. I mention it not in order to offer judgements about how things should have been done or received in that situation, but in order to kindle the reader's imagination that he may judge on this ticklish point of ecumenical good manners.

Many years ago now, the late Bernard Manning delivered an address to some students[1] which was the first essay in the

[1] *Some Lapsed Dissenters*, first published in the *Congregational Quarterly* for 1952, but delivered to the Cambridge University Congregational Society in 1930.

sociology of Dissent. It was also perhaps the most scarifying piece of satire that came from that graceful and versatile pen. One point there demonstrated is the extent to which it is assumed that Dissent betokens a lower degree of the class-ladder than Establishment. Dissent, in the language of a later generation, is non-U.

Historically Dissent is, of course, quite precisely non-U. It is not associated with the "upper classes." Neither is it associated with power. It is rare enough now for a politician or an eminent writer or an entertainer or anybody else greatly in the public eye to be a practising Nonconformist in religion; and rarer still for such a person to admit to Nonconformity otherwise than as part of a depressed past from which he has *ex-hypothesi* risen.

One consequence of this is very unpleasant. It is a tendency in Dissenters to be unduly sensitive to slights "from above." It is of no use for those who are deemed to be "above" to say that this is all nonsense. When a Dissenter finds himself in a parish church which is, compared to his own place, opulent in appointment, tasteful in manners, ceremonious in deportment, he feels somewhat as Mr. Doolittle feels in Professor Higgins's drawing-room. If he is articulate, as Doolittle, lively conversation can ensue. If he is not, he permits unacknowledged resentment to form in his mind, which appears only when he feels "slighted." Otherwise it commonly appears as the source of such judgements as—"I don't care for all this formality." In the case I have mentioned, the choir's gowns, the implied high standard of singing that the occasion was supposed to demand, the implied "you wouldn't be able to do this" caused offence in a Dissenting congregation: but this happened only because there was an underlying thought that the Establishment, represented by this august building and all its appurtenances, was assuming the inferiority of Dissent. That nothing could have been further from the mind of those who staffed the inviting church is beside the point.

It is of the utmost importance that this, the most powerful of all the non-theological factors in continuing disunity, be always kept in mind—especially by those who are in the position of the "inviting church," and can afford this much objectivity. In England, for example, Anglicans who are really disposed towards unity with Dissenters must be aware how much their rejection of Dissenting orders and closing of their altars to Dissenters has engendered a feeling of inferiority and resentment in Dissenting minds. It is not a straight disagreement between social equals. Dissent can see only too easily that the power and the finance, the public good manners, and good taste are all on the side of those who exclude them. They must try to be magnanimous enough to avoid being "Bolshie" about this; but those "above" must be very patient. Indeed, the one thing that has enabled Congregationalists to behave (when they do behave) properly and with a decent confidence in the presence of Anglicans is the fact that in certain fields where conversation has been on equal terms they have been able to show themselves a match for their opposite numbers: this notably in the field of scholarship, and latterly in ecumenical administration. Where any lack such ground of confidence, their manner in the presence of "those above" is bound to be somewhat aggressive, touchy and awkward. It will compensate itself by developing a vested interest in inferiority, by making more and more judgements about the undesirability of everything that pertains to "above-ness," by turning its back on any kind of ceremony, taste or discipline, by deriding the restraint that characterizes "established" worship as "dead formalism," by castigating the colour and adornment of such worship as vulgar display, and by saying that on the whole ministers and office-bearers of the Establishment are snobs. The pain which this gives to those who are doing all they can to avoid temptations of which they are well aware is enough to embitter relations between the great and the small, the top and the bottom, for good. But somehow this psychological and social disorder must patiently be overcome. It is now hardly present at all between ministers; but it is very much present among the rank and file, and in Congregationalism no less than in any other kind of Dissent.

### "The Course of True Love ..."

Practically, then, the difficulties in the way of unity are enormous. On the whole the present situation demands a good deal of clear, charitable and informed thinking at this practical level. Theological thinking we already have; and demonstrations of unity in all manner of ways we have—from New Delhi to Kirchentag. For good or ill we live in each other's pockets. Our young people attend the same universities and mix with one another and as often as not intermarry. A great deal of unofficial goodwill is shown in many English dioceses between clergy and ministers. Dissenting ministers appear now and again in cathedral pulpits. There is enough of this to make us feel that unity has made great progress in the last thirty years. But at the local level it is only too likely that frustration will set in when people begin to realize how fast the cause of unity is moving at one level, and how slowly it is moving at another.

Those of us who (like your present writer) minister in local churches in large cities must be prepared at any time for the call to unity to come in the form of a call to give up their security and their status. A minister of the Congregational order may be at this moment a person of some consequence in his own communion; in a larger, united communion he will be of less consequence. So will his elders. His actual church building may be closed and his congregation scattered or united with another. He may himself be, as it were, "out of a job." He may have to exchange his place of leadership for a place of assistantship. Even at the moment he has to face the question where, if the number of services held in his church is decreased because of movements in his locality towards unity, his maintenance is to come from. Suppose that a united church in England or Scotland has arrived at some sort of accommodation concerning orders and sacraments: what is to be the guiding principle concerning standards of culture and training in the ministry? He who might be received into one ministry might be debarred from another, and perhaps therefore from a united one, on the ground of insufficient training.

Fortunately, it is improbable that a union of the churches in our country would produce a positive redundancy of ministers. All the major communions complain of a shortage of ministers (probably Scottish Congregationalism is as well placed as any denomination in its ministerial supply).[1] The fear of having a number of middle-aged or senior men, unemployable in any other office, for whom provision must be made is not a very serious fear. In Congregationalism by far the most demanding adjustment is that which would have to be made between a tradition in which ministers work

[1] *Figures for* 1961–2: 145 churches, 119 ministers in pastoral charges, plus 41 ministers retired or in professional or secretarial posts. The figures are far less favourable in England. In 1959 they were: 3,023 churches, 1,246 ministers in pastoral charge, plus 458 retired or in professional or secretarial work.

alone, and one in which almost certainly they will have to work in teams. The economics and the ethos of Congregationalism have made its ministers lonely figures, at some times patriarchs of formidable isolation. The curate, the missioner, the canon, even the assistant minister, are unfamiliar figures. Community is not a Congregationalist pattern. This individualism, which very evidently is associated with the bourgeois provenance of the denomination as a whole, will have to undergo very serious adjustment, and since the ministry is to some extent moulded by this ethos, and gathers its recruits from men who tend to see their calling in the pattern of the lonely prophet rather than in that of the member of a community or team or priestly college, the whole notion of unity will appear unattractive to many of us. Once again—that cannot be helped. What matters is that those who claim to be free of psychological traits which in others they treat by turns with pity and exasperation shall use much imagination and liberality towards the healing of division.

I am assuming, of course, that a united church will involve much team-work among ministers. I cannot see any other possible pattern, unless it be envisaged that all ministers but those of a certain ecclesiastical background shall be excluded. Since I do not suppose for a moment that the controversial climate of 1593 or 1662 will be allowed to return, the evident necessity will be for the pooling of resources in local areas; and the initial steps towards such a consummation will be taken by full co-operation and team-work on the part of existing ministers. I repeat—in such measures it is not noticeable, for all their individualist tradition, that existing Congregationalists have been backward or unwilling to co-operate.

# 7

# Towards Asking the Real Question

## Congregationalists and Unity

CONGREGATIONALISTS, then, have lived through a history of four centuries which has brought them from the condition of extreme schismatics to a situation in which they are peculiarly well able to listen to, and to take part in, ecumenical conversations. At the beginning they were as fiercely exclusive as any Anabaptist; now they are supplying the world-wide work of the Church with a steady stream of scholars, administrators and leaders of religious experiment.

It is difficult to enlarge on this without appearing unduly complacent; but in fact there are few areas of modern religious life in which a Congregationalist, who began his career with a local ordination, is not to be found in a distinguished position. Confining myself to British Congregationalism, I can mention the associate secretary of the World Council of Churches (Dr. Leslie Cooke, ordained at Gatley, Lancs.), the Secretary of the International Missionary Council (Dr. Norman Goodall, Walthamstow), the Chairman of the Translation Committee of the New English

Bible New Testament (Professor C. H. Dodd, Warwick), the Reader in Divinity at the University of Durham (Dr. W. A. Whitehouse, Elland), the Editor of the United Society for Christian Literature (Dr. Cecil Northcott, St. Helens)—all of whom have emerged from the denominational interest of the Union to work in an ecumenical context: among those who have always held office within the Union but whose names are known far beyond its borders are Dr. Nathaniel Micklem (Bristol) and Dr. John Whale (Bowdon): the denomination has supplied enterprising younger men for short-term work with the Student Christian Movement, broadcasting and television, and for professorial chairs abroad (such as Dr. Horton Davies of Princeton, Dr. Robert Paul of Hartford, and Dr. George Caird who held chairs at Edmonton, Alberta and McGill, Montreal). All these—apart from men who have served and are now no longer with us, and men and women who in local pastorates or denominational colleges are ecumenical figures in their own right (such as, traditionally, the Minister of the Kings Weigh House, London, or the Principal of New College, London).

In earlier days, when Congregationalism was in more radical dissent from its neighbours, it produced its quota of eminent figures and picturesque characters, such as Dale of Birmingham, Joseph Parker of the City Temple (London), R. J. Campbell (once a Congregationalist, but at the end of his life an Anglican), and W. E. Orchard (who became a Roman Catholic); in days when Scottish Congregationalism preserved a high tradition of scholarship, it produced Alexander Souter, editor of the first Oxford Text of the New Testament, and (from its Evangelical Union side) A. M. Fairbairn, the first Principal of Mansfield College.

All this is worth mentioning only to contrast the present-day movement into ecumenicity with the movement away from it which was the first impulse of primitive Congregationalism. Another decisive influence in turning Congregationalists away from the interests of mere schism was the missionary movement of the late eighteenth century; and although the London Missionary Society is now so closely associated with the Congregational churches as to be the subject at present of negotiations for integration with the Union, at its inception Congregationalists were associated on equal terms with evangelically-minded Anglicans; its foundation, therefore, had the double effect of giving expression to the new concern for the unconverted that was arising in the churches, and of showing that co-operation with the Church of England was far from being the impossible proposition which it had appeared to be.

Incentives towards unity have been neither lacking nor without response in Congregationalism; and yet in Britain there have been no successful movements towards union with any of the Free Church denominations. It is far otherwise in Canada and America, in both of which places the word "Congregationalist" has now disappeared, with the merging of Congregational churches in wider Protestant denominations. In Canada the dominating influence in the United Church is Presbyterian, in America, Evangelical. It may be noted, however, that in the U.S.A., although Congregationalism was the faith of the founding fathers, the differences between its ethos and that which developed in its English counterpart were so wide as to alter radically the conditions of its relations with other groups. Although in America there has never been a state church, there was undoubtedly (in the modern sense) a Congregational

Establishment in Massachusetts, represented by the "old families." Church Meeting has never had the significance in the U.S.A. that it has had here. Grievances against "those above" have been entirely absent. Historic roots of dissents have been shallower; denominational differences both less theological and less socially complicated.

I do not think it is my business here to answer at length the question which many ask—why, in these ecumenical days, there has been no union of the Free Churches in this country: that is a subject for a book on Free Churches (and the best source for its study is E. K. H. Jordan's *Free Church Unity*, Lutterworth, 1956). But briefly—between Congregationalists and Baptists, who share their church-polity and much of their culture and sense of enterprise, there is the dogmatic barrier of believers' baptism, which has blocked any approach to union. Between Congregationalists and Presbyterians (in England) there are certain practical difficulties, including the ministry of women and the form of church government, which have prevented the two unions coming closer together than is implied in the recent declaration of covenant-relationship (1948) and the more recent statement concerning the interavailability of ministers. Methodism stands in a peculiar relationship to its Free Church sisters, in being historically not so much a dissent as a mission, seeing itself traditionally vis-à-vis the Church of England more as the Jesuits saw themselves vis-à-vis the papacy than as Protestants saw themselves. Its special form of organization, its government by Conference, its tradition of short and powerful ministries have placed Methodism on a different plane from other Free Churches, and it has proved in practice peculiarly difficult for either side, as between Congregationalism and Methodism, to see what they or the others would gain by union. Methodism has recently shown much more interest in conversation with the Church of England: and this is natural, because its departure from that Church was an historically unwilling departure, not a defiant one. Congregationalists in the rank and file have often found themselves culturally nearer the Wesleyan wing of Methodist, and ritually nearer the Primitive wing; and in some quarters the developing relations between "Wesleyans" and the Church of England have discouraged conversation between Methodism and Congregationalists of the "Primitive" sort.

Apart from such public action as has been possible by the Free Church Federal Council, comprising all these denominations, the English Free Churches have not much to show in the way of ecumenical development. Perhaps the Calvinist Dissenters (Free Churches without Methodists) have not yet found an impulse to unity which will replace that negative impulse which a common fear and hatred of Anglicanism, but for the ecumenical movement, might have provided.

But there is this somewhat vexatious fact which emerges from any discussion of Free Church unity—that the smaller the two parties to a discussion of unity, the longer are the odds against the success of any such discussions. Consider the example of Scotland. In 1843, at the Disruption, one very large body of Christians broke away from the Kirk, and established itself as the Free Kirk of Scotland. It had power, money and influence enough to make it from that time a competitor on equal terms. Therefore when the time came for the healing of the breach, the conversations were on equal terms, with on either side men of equally formidable mind and conscience. But further—on either side were men of equally wide vision and theological concern for the Church. Therefore when the healing of the breach came in 1929 it was a massive gesture of reconciliation, and has proved a genuine and lasting union. The legacy of 1843 is still an undesirable plurality of church buildings, but on the whole there is very little left in the *ex*-Free Kirk or the *ex*-Kirk of Scotland to show their denominational provenance.

Now take the Evangelical Union and the Congregationalists, who merged in 1896. Neither was a large denomination. The "E.U." (as it is always known in Scotland) was formed in 1843 after the suspension of a Scottish minister (James Morison) two years earlier for theology distasteful to Calvinists. The Scottish Congregational Union was an evangelical movement begun at the end of the eighteenth century independent of the Kirk of Scotland. These two bodies, which had always worked closely together, united in 1896. To this day, Congregational churches of "E.U." provenance always state the fact on their notice-boards, and retain a different church order (without church meeting) from that followed by "primitive" Scottish Congregationalists. The cultures have rarely merged at all.

The small dissenting denominations in Scotland continue in stubborn isolation: when two Secession splinter groups, the United Secession Church (1820) and the Relief Synod formed in 1847 the United Presbyterian Church, and the United Presbyterian Church in turn merged with the Free Kirk to form the United Free Church in 1900, the "Wee Frees," as they came to be called, kept out of the union. When the United Free Church returned to the Church of Scotland in 1929, certain of its members and ministers declined to associate themselves with the union, and a small body remains which is known as the United Free Church. Between these small groups there is at present no thought of ecumenical encounter. Although the "U.F." church works closely with Congregationalism in Scotland at one level—sharing a theological college—there is more interest among Congregationalists than in the U.F. in conversations with the Kirk.

It will always be so. Any united church will leave certain dissents which continue over short or long periods. This fact brings us near to our final question, which I venture to call the real question about Dissent.

### The Real Question

We are bound to ask, I believe, whether we can reliably distinguish between controversy and schism. This prepares us to answer the question—Is schism a sin?

It may have occurred to the reader that a great deal of what I have written here is beside the point. It is clearly beside the point that was urged in my opening chapter. I want now to state what I believe to be the present consequence of the mental muddle of which my argument up to this point is—intentionally—a symbol. I appear to have started out on the assumption that unity is one thing, and then written fifty pages on the assumption that it is another.

Allow me first to give an illustration of the answer which I would urge on my fellow-Christians.

When I was at my theological college, we were a small number of students: about sixteen, for it was wartime. Among these was a great diversity of background, theological temper, and world-view. In particular I remember that there was one group which was especially engaged by a theology derived from Barth; and another that was equally engaged by a theology derived from St. Thomas Aquinas through the (then) recent English Catholic theological revival. Debate continued between members of these groups on many levels, from the friendly leg-pull to the profound conversation over late-night coffee. I do not recall any occasion on which this debate became acrimonious, although every theological point of importance presented itself in a different way to those who were committed to one of the two experimental opinions. Every conversation reflected the debate, but it was friendly.

Later experience of theological colleges has introduced me to a situation far different. I have encountered in more than one place student-bodies divided in a condition varying from helpless silence to open rancour between those who hold, and those who do not hold, a conservative-evangelical view of the Bible and of theology. I raise the matter here only to use as an illustration the difference between a controversy that remains friendly, though both parties to it are committed, and one which becomes acrid and separates men from one another. It happens to be a fact at present that the dispute concerning the conservative-evangelical position has opened a rift in the church deeper than that caused by any denominational difference except that between Protestants and Roman Catholics in Liverpool or Glasgow. Everybody knows this, and there is no need to labour it here.

What here concerns me is the difference between a counterpoint of views which enhances the joy that people find in each other's company, and a clash which robs them of the chance of finding any such joy. This is the most important of all the distinctions that must be kept in the minds of those who plan ecumenical affairs.

If then we are to shift our whole argument back into the key in which our opening chapter was written, we must now ask, of what possible use to the kingdom of God would be a united church in Great Britain, or even in England.

A united church could be united in the same manner in which people who are in the same room together and say no word to one another are united; or in which those are united who speak only in conventionalities. Or it could be united in the sense in which a fascist state is united. Or it could be united in the way in which propaganda for religious revivals commonly suggests unity—in an enthusiastic, automatic and conditioned assent to the words of some leader or committee of leaders, all united in one comprehensive beaming smile.

Such unions are contemptible. If anybody achieves such a union he will deceive himself into thinking he had achieved much, when in fact he has set the kingdom back a thousand years.

I invite my reader to consider a question whose answer I cannot give (for neither have I enough evidence, nor has enough time passed); this is the question to what extent the united churches of our time have proved to be lively vehicles of the Gospel, effective and economical instruments of evangelism, centres of missionary revolution, powerhouses of radical dissent from the values of the world. How far in history has "merger" contributed to the success of those values which "division" was held to be impeding? It is too early yet to find the answer—but not too early to subject existing unions to continuing scrutiny. It could be (in no case am I saying that it is) that a united church became an entrenchment of complacency, a monolithic stronghold of conservatism, an efficient and well-run crematorium for the values of the Gospel.

But if a vigilant eye is kept on that kind of question, it will emerge that we stand in danger of thinking too facilely about the "sin of schism." I find in too few contemporary documents and books on this subject a recognition of the dynamic difference between a controversy that is schism and a controversy that is growth.

Controversy is not sin. It is bad theology to say that it is. Disagreement is not sin. "Where is disunity and sinful division? Is it in the fact that members of one communion cannot meet at the Lord's Table with members of another? That is not sin: it is sin's sorry consequence, but it is not sin. Here is sin exposed—when at the Armistice Day service in the parish church the Methodist minister is invited to read the Lesson and the Congregationalist is offended because he was not invited. . . . The seeds of that disunity which is wholly displeasing to God and which continues the suffering of the Crucified are not organizational difficulties or technical disputes, but the ancient sins to which all men are heirs, pride, wrath, greed, fear of the truth, fear of losing face, self-love and the rest.' Trusting that the reader will forgive the repetition of words that I wrote seven years ago,[1] I repeat them, and state that I believe them to be the truth. In our present enthusiasm for New Delhi and all that it stands for, and in our present economic embarrassments which make the continuance of the denominations a more hazardous thing than it was in our grandfathers' time, we are still short of authoritative guidance on the difference between unity for prudence's sake and unity in Christ's name.

[1] *Hymns and the Faith* (John Murray, 1955), p. 245.

Let us suppose then that there are two kinds of unity—an outward unity which is of prudence and of the law, and an inward unity which is of joy and of grace: what kind of visible unity ought we to seek and to make sacrifices for?

The real unity is the pleasure that people take in one another. To achieve this, people must be persons. To be persons they must be individually developed, alert and confident, and also social creatures, aware of and rejoicing in the demands that society makes on them. They must increase in "the Courage to Be" and in charity.

Joy does not come by lawgiving; you cannot, indeed, advise or persuade men into joy any more than you can compel them into it. Therefore there is no church system which realizes this ideal fully and which can be built up by men, be they never so patient or wise. We believe that it is the Holy Spirit's intention that this unity shall be expressed in His Church; but when we speak of men's organizing or lawgiving, we are speaking not of architects but at best of demolition-contractors.

What must be demolished? I have already answered that to some extent in relation to Congregationalism. Much in the way of vested interest must go. But dissent in charity must not go. Remembering in penitence that throughout the Church's history the creative moments have been moments of dissent, and the great breakings-through of evangelism have been the acts of men upon which Establishments looked as disturbers of the peace (Loyola, Luther, Wesley, Livingstone, Temple—but the line goes back to the Apostle Paul); remembering the limitless capacity of the human heart for deceiving itself and especially for confusing what is prudent with what is the will of the Lord—remembering these things, and never allowing them out of our mind's sight, let us talk of unity.

Unity has come spectacularly in works of charity. The Inter-Church Aid and Refugee Department of the World Council of Churches is the greatest single argument in existence against those who say that the Church is irretrievably hamstrung by its divisions. The collaboration of Protestants and Catholics in works of mercy is now an understood and accepted thing. When the situation in which the Good Samaritan found himself is before them, Christians forget their dissents. But Christians have not learnt yet that they have a right, given them by Christ, to seek joy in one another. They have learnt well that they have a duty to relieve suffering: they have not learnt of the right to seek joy and promote it.

It is in this sense that a Congregationalist can, *qua* Congregationalist, urge the demands and the splendours of unity on his co-religionists. Unity that means the suppression of minority views will always be abhorrent to his communion. But a communion which has that in its history and tradition which places so high a value on the joy of the *koinonia* ought to be implacably opposed to the continuance of any Dissent that is based on blindness, conservatism, the unwillingness to speak or to answer, or the unwillingness to meet the present-day world's demands. To continue any Dissent which is based on the hope of avoiding the necessity to repent is an offence to that charity which rejoices in the truth.

At this moment in our history Congregationalists can claim that they have been called to a reappraisal of all their traditions, to a rediscovery of the principles of liturgy, theology and churchmanship. As I write, men are earnestly conferring in our Central Offices, at the bidding of their leaders, on matters of the deepest theological and practical concern. If Congregationalism is rehabilitating its corporate "personality," regaining confidence, discovering a new articulacy, learning to live with itself, it is also learning to live with its neighbours. This is the moment when Congregationalists can speak freely with others, and listen without anxiety to the questions of others. But it is clearly our duty not only to hasten on with the work of clearing obsolete and useless prejudices out of the way, and tearing down all life-expired structures of faith and practice; but also to cultivate among ourselves the pursuit of joy; that when it comes to asking the great questions, we may be hindered by no hatred, contempt, inverted snobbery or anxious pride.

I write this in the belief, which I trust is not over-optimistic, that we are ready now to take the first steps towards asking the real question.

# APPENDIX

## A CONGREGATIONAL STATEMENT OF BELIEF CONCERNING THE CHURCH MEETING, IN A MODERN ECUMENICAL CONTEXT

THIS is quoted from the Introduction to the report of the General Committee of the Congregational Union of Scotland on the progress of conversations with the Church of Scotland; it is to be found in the *Year Book of the Congregational Union of Scotland for* 1962–3, p. 34.

Congregationalists emphasize the importance of the Local Church and make great claims for it. Perhaps the most characteristic of these is the autonomy of the Local Church. The term is not easy to define. Usually, autonomy is thought of as independency from outside interference and full freedom to manage the internal affairs of the Local Church. Congregationalists live and work together harmoniously on that basis and have a strong sense of fellowship with one another. But as soon as any attempt is made to be precise as to what is meant by "independence from outside interference," and "full freedom," then differences in emphasis appear. But despite the differences, there is agreement on the principle that the autonomy claimed by the Local Church is not an end in itself, but is a means towards a proper obedience to the Lord Jesus Christ. The autonomy thus claimed is a spiritual principle by means of which the Local Church acknowledges the Lordship of Jesus Christ. This means that the Local Church exists to serve Christ and not just itself. Further, it is on the basis of an autonomy understood in this sense that Congregationalists emphasize the central importance of the Church Meeting. Through this meeting, the Local Church provides an opportunity for the Church members to meet for the specific purpose of seeking the guidance of the Holy Spirit in the work the Lord is calling them to do. It is true, of course, that the Church Meeting is not always used as it ought to be. Nevertheless it is an essential and integral part of the Local

Church's way of life and witness. In its regular, practical use in the Local Church, it offers justification for the claim to autonomy under Jesus Christ.

The Church of Scotland would agree that the emphasis which is laid by Congregationalists upon the value of regular meetings of the congregation for the purpose of seeking God's guidance upon subjects of Christian concern, both within its own life and within the community, is a perfectly correct one. The Congregation is the body of Christ within the parish, and as such must endeavour in every way possible to understand and fulfil the responsibility laid upon it by its very existence within the will and purpose of God. . . . In the Church of Scotland system, provision is made for the calling of meetings of the Congregation for the purpose of honouring such responsibilities.

In the course of conversations it became clear that it is in the area of our understanding of the Lordship of Jesus over His Church that the differences in attitude to the Local Church as between the Church of Scotland and the Congregationalists can be lessened or even overcome. The autonomy of the Local Church leads the Congregationalists to ascribe authority to the Local Church, whereas the Church of Scotland ascribes authority to the General Assembly. But the General Assembly, no less than the Local Church, makes this claim in order to be free to acknowledge the Lordship of Jesus Christ. Both are equally under one and the same Lord, and both seek to be obedient to Him.

The above statement can be placed alongside the conviction which is implicit in the minds of most Congregationalists that their annual Assembly, and County or District Union meetings, operate under precisely the same doctrine of authority that governs the Church Meeting.

OOKS ON CON

HISTORY

T. Jones: *Congregationalism in E* 1962).

E. Routley: *The Story of Con*

A. G. Matthews (ed.): *The* Press, 1958).

DOCTRINE

J. Huxtable (ed.): *The True* 1655) (Independent Press, 1947)

N. Micklem: *Congregationalism* Press, 1943).

CULTURE AND CRITICISM

D. T. Jenkins: *Congregationalism—a Restatement* (Faber, 1954).

B. Manning: *Essays in Orthodox Dissent* (Independent Press, 1942).

SPECIAL CHAPTERS AND ARTICLES

B. Manning: "Some Lapsed Dissenters" (*Congregational Quarterly*, 1952).

D. T. Jenkins: *The Protestant Ministry* (Faber, 1958: esp. chs. 1–5).

C. J. Cadoux and T. T. James: *The Congregational Way* (Blackwell, paper, 1945).

SPECIALIST BOOKS

A. Peel and L. H. Carlson (ed.): *The Writings of Robert Browne and Robert Harrison* (1950).

L. H. Carlson (ed.): *The Writings of Henry Barrow and John Greenwood* (1962) (both in the series, "Elizabethan Nonconformist Texts," Allen & Unwin, of which more are in preparation).

ECUMENICAL

R. F. G. Calder: *To Introduce the Family* (Independent Press, 1953: a short account of International Congregationalism).

E. J. Price: *Baptists, Congregationalists and Presbyterians* (Independent Press, paper, 1953).

N. Micklem: *Facts* (Independent Press, 1946) a report on preliminary discussions between Congregationalists and Presbyterians).

N. Micklem and V. McNab: *Catholics and Nonconformists* (Catholic Truth Society pamphlet, 1942).

P. T. Forsyth: *Congregationalism and Reunion* (Independent Press, 1952—first printed, 1917).